WHAT SUCCESSFUL PEOPLE DO IN SOCIAL MEDIA

A Short Guide to Boosting Your Career

by Caroline Leach

Editing by Cat Spydell
Cover design by Janice Walters
Photography by Jessica Sterling

DEDICATION

*To my grandmother, Graer Kate,
my parents, Chris and Harvey,
and my husband, Kevin,
who believed in me
and encouraged me
every step of the way*

ABOUT THIS BOOK

In *What Successful People Do in Social Media*, I will share with you real-life examples and a growing body of research as I teach you what the most successful people do in social media to build their careers and companies.

You will learn about the power of personal branding—what it is, why it's imperative in today's world, and how to build a compelling brand for yourself.

You will learn which social networks to invest your time in, how to build a broad and diverse network, and what content to share to establish yourself as a thought leader in your field.

Using the techniques I've learned over the last decade, I will also show you how to give back to others and help you, your colleagues, and your companies succeed.

For more than a dozen years, I was a vice president of Corporate Communications and Marketing at Fortune 100 companies. On New Year's Day 2015, I launched a blog about the future of corporate communications. My blog evolved into an exploration of how professionals boost their careers through social media.

Now I write, research, consult, speak, and teach about what successful people do in social media. In this book, I give you the roadmap to achieve your own career dreams, one post at a time.

CONTENTS

CHAPTER 1

Successful People Have a Social Media Strategy for Their Career

As the pace of change in the world accelerates, how do you boost your career growth? How do you build a vibrant professional network? How do you show your hard-won expertise? How do you keep learning?

The answers can be found in the power of social media. Making an investment of time into growing your network, creating and curating content, and learning about your industry can raise your visibility and accelerate your career progress. Yet we often hear about the downside of social media—inappropriate posts that lead to damaged reputations and lost jobs.

You may remember the PR person who tweeted an offensive comment before a long intercontinental flight. Or perhaps you heard about the Facebook rant by a corporate lawyer after a mass shooting. Then there was a post by an elected official criticizing the participants in the Women's March.

The PR person was fired before the flight landed. The corporate lawyer was let go within hours of the post. The elected official was defeated by a candidate who was motivated to enter the race by the post and its aftermath.

These are just a few examples of how bad behavior on social media can get you into serious trouble. I've seen some ill-advised posts myself. One person wrote that they didn't intend to be with their company in a year. Another person posted an internal company memo to employees. Still others make their content all about themselves, turning off members of their networks.

But what about the upside? How can social media help build and boost your career? How can it accelerate your progress to increasing levels of responsibility?

The dilemma reminds me of the brain-bending question, "If a tree falls in a forest but no one is around to hear it, does it make a sound?"

In your work you could launch a game-changing product, provide a life-changing customer experience, or create an awe-inspiring place to work. But if other people don't know about it, you won't reach your full potential in the workplace.

Here's some eye-opening data. About 95% of recruiters use LinkedIn to vet candidates, according to Money magazine.[1] That's a staggering number, although it does make me wonder how the other 5% are reviewing candidates!

A positive social media presence can boost your prospects. Forty-four percent of employers have found social media content that caused them to hire a candidate,[2] according to a CareerBuilder survey by The Harris Poll of hiring managers and HR professionals.

And if you believe it may be safer to avoid social media and have no presence whatsoever, that can be a red flag to some companies. About half of employers are *less* likely to interview someone they can't find online, according to the CareerBuilder survey.

In the last year, nearly every person I know from their twenties to their fifties who got a new job said the same thing. They weren't necessarily looking, but a recruiter found them on LinkedIn. One conversation led to another, and the next thing they knew, they were starting a great new job that moved their career to a higher level.

My nephew, Kodiak Spydell, landed a job at an architecture firm because of a comment he made on a friend's Instagram post. That led the friend to mention she was leaving her job. She asked if Kodiak would be interested in exploring it as her replacement. He took the job and made a big impact while he was there.

These are just a few examples of why you need a social media strategy for your career.

Think of it as having "social savvy"—the vital ability for you to personally brand and market yourself in social media in our ever-evolving world. Being savvy in your social media creates three big opportunities for you.

First, you can build a diverse and vibrant network of professional relationships. Even in our technology-fueled world, most things still get done through personal relationships, whether it's being considered for a new job or a consulting project.

Second, you can become a thought leader in your field or in a new area of interest and position yourself for career opportunities. Simply by sharing content on a consistent and thoughtful basis, people will come to see you as an expert.

Third, you can accelerate your learning and development by reading and viewing content relevant to your career field. As lifespans and careers lengthen, this is an efficient, effective and fun way to become a lifelong learner.

An Ah-ha Moment

What got me thinking about how social media can help build your career? I was listening to Reese Witherspoon, the actor, producer and entrepreneur.

Reese spoke at a leadership event I attended a few years ago. With more than 17 million Instagram followers as of this writing, she was asked about her success with social media. She talked about the importance of authenticity and of being herself.

Then she made the comment that changed my life. She talked about social media content creation for individuals to shape their reputations and images. "It's a big white space that's not fully filled," she said.

Her comment became my personal *Legally Blonde* moment. A gasp. An 'a-ha.' Like when her character Elle Woods decided, "I think I'll go to law school."

Yet in my case it was, "I think I'll change my blog."

The realization made me connect some dots. I love to help people tell their stories. I'm endlessly fascinated by social media, with its connection and communication power. And people often ask me for help with it.

So I refocused my blog. It originally began on New Year's Day 2015 as an exploration of the future of corporate communications. At the time I was a vice president of that area at DIRECTV, a Fortune 100 entertainment and technology company.

The VP role was a career goal of mine ever since I got my master's degree in communications management from the University of Southern California Annenberg School for Communication and Journalism. Happily, I landed the VP position after a decade in the field. In retrospect, I wonder if social media had existed at the time if I could have further fast-tracked my career. But that's a story for another time.

The beloved company I worked for was acquired a few years ago by a new company in the technology, media and telecommunications arena. I had the opportunity of a lifetime to be part of the merger integration planning team. When the deal closed, I was offered a VP role in marketing analytics.

If moving from corporate communications to marketing analytics seems like a stretch, I can say it was an upside to the acquisition. It was a fairly dramatic shift from working with words and people in corporate communications to dealing with data and numbers in marketing analytics and research. It wasn't something I would have been able to do easily in the original beloved company. In the research arena, I *had* overseen the employee engagement survey strategy as well as studies on what defined the company's culture. I quickly riffled through my files at home to find my notes from the one graduate school class I took on communication research.

For a while I explored marketing analytics in my blog. Ever since I took career blogger Penelope Trunk's online class about reaching your goals through blogging, I shared her view that blogging is a way to learn something new, including an industry or a career field.

Sadly, though, I discovered my heart wasn't into devoting extensive weekend and evening hours to writing and learning about marketing analytics. Looking at numbers all day about brand and advertising trends didn't spark my interest the way I hoped it would. I was a word and idea person who was now spending my time poring over charts and graphs of data and numbers.

But I *was* fascinated by how people learn and how people accelerate the learning process. That's what I was doing in my new role every day, trying to keep up with a steep learning curve as I slogged through early mornings and late nights to quickly learn a language of a new and different function.

There was no time for my weekend blogging, and I no longer knew what to write about. I was stuck. If you see a theme here, it's that I wasn't really sure of the direction I wanted my blog to go. I just knew I loved to write, as I had since I was five years old and my uncle gave me a typewriter (younger readers can Google what this is). I enjoyed being in the flow state of connecting ideas and sharing thoughts. The cares of the world would melt away and I felt fully engaged with the interplay of ideas in my mind. Yet I was in search of a blog topic that would make the hours of my free time that I devoted to it worthwhile. It felt almost as unsettling as when I graduated from college and wondered what I should do next. The parallels were striking.

That's why Reese Witherspoon's comment was so life changing. I was a person desperately searching for a new direction. And her words turned on a light.

Enter Social Savvy

In my very first blog post on New Year's Day 2015, I asked the question I mentioned earlier in this chapter: "If a company or a person does something great but no one knows about it, does it really matter?" The analogy of the tree falling in the woods with no one around to hear it was hidden in those words.

Sometimes, random acts of kindness are intended to be under the radar. Yet, hearing about them can be inspiring when others share the news, like my sister Katie Rogers did on Facebook.

While getting coffee in her Connecticut town, she overhead another customer buying a gift card for the police officer outside who was directing traffic. That's an instant day brightener. And maybe it will inspire others toward similar acts of kindness.

Data and information are collected about us every day, according to *The Reputation Economy* by Michael Fertik.[3] A few examples are where we go, who we associate with, and what we say on social media. The question is what we *want* that data to say about us as a person and as a professional.

Do we want it to open doors or close them? Do we want it to augment the hard work we do every day or detract from it? Do we want it to make our life better or make it harder?

More and more, everything we do has implications for our own personal reputations as well as the companies where we work or that we own. This occurs in both our real lives, as well as how we are represented in social media.

What it all means is that we each have great power to do good in the world, to a larger extent than has ever been available to us. And it also means we have the potential to make major missteps.

That is why each of us needs to have social savvy— the vital ability for people to personally brand and market themselves successfully in social media in our ever-evolving world.

This skill is important throughout our lives. It applies to high-school students who are preparing their college applications or moving into the working world.

It applies to college and grad school students who are getting ready to transition into the working world. It applies to people throughout their professional lives as they navigate new projects, new jobs, and new career fields.

For corporate professionals in particular, the stakes for social media are higher. Social media can help or hurt careers. It can add to or detract from a corporate reputation and an employer brand, the promise about what it's like to work at a particular company. It can make acquiring top talent a breeze or a burden.

The risks are vast. But so are the rewards. In our ever-changing world, no one can afford to sit on the sidelines. The pace of change is too fast. It seems like just yesterday that Snapchat was the darling of younger generations, but Instagram is now edging ahead of Snapchat among teens.[4]

Corporate professionals often ignore or short-change social media. Why? They don't have the time, they don't see the value, and they don't want to make a mistake.

ABC cancelled the hit sitcom "Roseanne" shortly after Roseanne Barr sent a derogatory tweet about a top political aide.[5] She lost the show that she created, while her television family moved on without her in a new show.

In college sports, the Washington State football coach's tweet of a fake video of a former U.S. President may have led the university to lose $1.6 million in donations, according to a school official.[6]

The opposite end of this spectrum is developing social savvy. With a positive approach to social media, professionals can create and implement a social strategy to highlight and share their own thought processes and achievements, along with those of their organizations.

Social savvy is a powerful way for corporate professionals to build their personal brand, advance their career, and embrace their future. It applies well beyond the corporate world to anyone who wants to make a name for themselves and share their perspectives on who they are and what they do. A college student, a stay-at-home parent, a community volunteer, or a retired person are all examples of people outside the corporate world who could use these strategies to further their goals.

What are some examples of social savvy? It's using social media to build and amplify your personal brand, the unique value that you bring to the world. It's positioning yourself in the most favorable light, for a number of career and life paths.

It's showing your employer or company in the most favorable light. It's advancing your career through a positive social strategy. It's helping others boost their careers. It's building your employer's corporate reputation and employer brand.

It's knowing what to do and not to do in social media. It's seeing the links between real life and social savvy. And it's knowing when and how to engage with critics. These are the secrets I'll share with you in *What Successful People Do in Social Media*.

Why People are Active in Social Media Professionally

Why and how people use social media to build their careers is a big area of curiosity for me. It was among several questions I set out to answer in research I conducted. There's plenty of anecdotal evidence by simply observing what people are posting on the platforms—mainly LinkedIn and Twitter, followed by Instagram and Facebook. But we live in a data-driven world, and numbers are important. So I ran a survey on the subject in the spring of 2018.[7]

As I often tell the students I mentor, some of what I learned in graduate school is surprisingly timeless in our fast-changing world. One of those evergreen courses is "Uses of Communications Research," which I revisit on occasion.

One thing that *has* changed a lot is expansion of the functionality of research platforms such as Survey Monkey. In creating my study on the Survey Monkey website, the process felt gamified in a fun way, meaning there were elements of playing a game while I wrote my survey. As one example, I kept editing the survey until the platform gave a perfect score of 100% for the structure of the questions.

The main goal of my research was to learn how fellow professionals are using social media to build their careers. Specifically, it addressed what social media people use professionally and personally, why they are active on social media professionally, and how their social media activity has helped their career, others' careers and their employer. My intent is to conduct the survey annually to view trends over time, as the Social Media Study of Professionals.

More than 100 people responded, with about 80% being employed full time and 20% owning a business. Of all the respondents, more than 10% ran a side gig, or an activity that people get paid to do in addition to their main job. Nearly half were Generation X, about 30% were Millennials, and just under 20% were Baby Boomers.

When I asked why people are active in social media to boost their careers, they could choose as many answers as applied. The top three reasons were to build a network, access news about their industry and profession, and learn continually about their industry and profession.

Responses that were lower down the list than I expected were finding a new job, establishing thought leadership, raising visibility among key decision makers at an employer, positioning oneself for a promotion, and changing careers.

It surprised me that thought leadership wasn't higher. Because social media offers such a significant opportunity to share content and establish expertise, I hope and expect to see this number grow in the future.

In fact, it could even be considered the flip side of learning continually about your industry and profession. In the comments, many respondents wrote that they sought out and followed thought leaders for continual learning. Here's what a few said:

> *"I follow key leaders within my company on LinkedIn and Twitter, as well as best-selling authors and speakers and influential business men and women to know what's happening in our industry, but also to learn career advice that will help anyone regardless of industry."*

> *"I read articles daily on LinkedIn to find out more about my industry and learn about other industries I'm interested in."*

> *"I follow several thought leaders on social media*

> *... and they help me expand my horizons and my thinking, hopefully to the benefit of my entire team!"*

With so many people looking to social media to continually learn new information that's relevant to their career and industry, that creates an opportunity for you.

If you need compelling reasons to start establishing yourself as a thought leader, here they are. People are seeking thought leaders, we all need to learn continually, and you have insights to share. When you share them, you learn yourself, contribute to your network, and start to establish yourself as an expert.

And just as we learn through social media, I learned a great deal conducting this first survey in a series. One thing is that social media for career building is in its early days, which creates opportunity. Although 98% of respondents are on LinkedIn and 47% are on Twitter for professional use, some of the comments told a different story. "I use social media personally, not professionally," wrote one respondent. "I don't really use social media to build my career. I see social media as just that, social," said another.

My conclusion is that these are the nascent days for social media and careers. At first, this disappointed me. But the flip side is the big opportunity for all of us. This is especially true for people navigating transitions to new jobs.

This brings us full circle to the CareerBuilder data that 70% of employers use social media to screen candidates, 57% of employers are less likely to interview a candidate they can't find online, and 44% have found social media content that caused them to hire a candidate.

People follow thought leaders in social media to learn, which creates opportunity. Among the top reasons for being active in social media professionally, learning was continually cited by 77% of respondents. In comments, people said they followed thought leaders as part of their learning agenda.

Whether you realize it or not, you have a unique and valuable perspective on your profession and your industry. By sharing that in social media, one post at a time, you can establish yourself as a thought leader and an expert.

Bestselling author and marketing strategist Dorie Clark talks about the importance of content creation in her Harvard Business Review article, What You Need to Stand Out in a Noisy World. "The fact that you're the one creating content, rather than simply quoting others," she says, "makes you an expert in many people's eyes."[8]

Of course, the caveat is that you should *never* share confidential or proprietary information about your employer. When in doubt, ask for the advice of your supervisor or err on the side of caution and don't share.

Actor and former NFL player Terry Crews reminds us about the power of your unique voice. In his interview with author Tim Ferriss for the book *Tribe of Mentors*, Terry says, "When you're creative, you render the competition obsolete, because there is only one you, and no one can do things exactly the way you do."[9]

No one has had your unique experience, and no one can write about it the way you can. If that sounds daunting, you can start with small steps. I call them experiments. Try sharing your perspective in a social media post in LinkedIn or Twitter. See what resonates with your audience, and tweak your approach as appropriate.

Keep at it long enough to gain some traction. Here I'm inspired by author Tim Ferriss. As a fledgling writer, he received dozens of book rejections. Thank goodness he persisted with his first book, *The Four-Hour Work Week*, a perennial bestseller about moving beyond the 9 to 5 world. We get the benefit of his learning as a result.

Observing others and experimenting are the ways to learn and improve. My social media survey was a form of observing others and seeing what works for them. Another approach is engaging with my social feeds in LinkedIn, Twitter, Instagram, and Facebook.

What You'll Learn in this Book

Now that you know *why* successful people use social media to build and boost their careers, let's turn to what the rest of the book will cover. In meeting a potential client for coffee recently, she asked me where to get the book or the class that would teach her everything we walked through. I have long been sharing this information in my blog, post by post. But rather than simply say to people that they can read through nearly 200 blog posts and try to figure it all out, I'm bringing that material along with new and fresh content together in a series of books.

This book and others to come will also distill what I've spoken to many groups about on the fundamentals of social media for career building. This is the foundational book that will cover the big picture of how you can use social media to boost your career. As I mentioned earlier, people beyond the corporate world can also use these principles to achieve the goals they have for their particular life role at the moment.

Chapter 2 will look at the three big trends that will define careers now and in the future. They are globalization, technology, and demographics. Each is a powerful force shaping our professional and personal lives. They also interact to produce an even stronger effect on the trajectory of your future.

Chapter 3 addresses the professional and personal blend in social media and how to get it right for you. It covers different approaches, discusses the pros and cons of each, and makes the case that we all have one life that is the brand known as you. You'll learn why it's the most efficient to have a blended approach to content that is suitable for all audiences.

Chapter 4 helps you articulate your personal brand by deciding who you want to be, looking at how people already perceive you, and refining the brand that is you. Creating a personal brand is one of the top work skills of the future. This chapter will show you how do develop a compelling and successful brand.

Chapter 5 gives you a decision matrix for which social networks to use to boost your career. A personal blog is a strong starting point. LinkedIn is the clear choice after that, with Twitter a close second. There's a role for Instagram and Facebook, too, and you'll understand the reasoning behind it in this chapter. You'll also learn how to view the platforms holistically for your career.

Chapter 6 tells you everything you need to know to build your network over time. It shows why a diverse network of both close and loose ties is important. It explains how the mantra to always be connecting actually works on a daily basis. And it demonstrates how reciprocity in social media adds to the value of your carefully curated network.

Chapter 7 is all about content creation and how to establish yourself as a thought leader. The most compelling and engaging content for your network is both creative and innovative at the same time it is speculative, where you're continually experimenting and trying new things to see what resonates the most with people.

Chapter 8 is about the guiding principles of your social media approach. Consistency is rewarded in social media by more followers and more engagement. Persistence is necessary for those times when you wonder if the investment of time in your social media efforts is worth it. Efficiency is what makes it all manageable.

Chapter 9 covers how to achieve the social media trifecta of promoting yourself, your colleagues, and your company all at the same time. This increases your network's engagement with your content and promotes your employer's brand, or how they're seen by potential job candidates and current employees as a good place to work.

Chapter 10 brings it all together by showing you how to fit social media for career building into your everyday life. There are time hacks you can easily work into your day as well as technology solutions that can automate some of what you do. You'll learn how to handle haters, manage the volume of incoming messages, and use social media to become the best version of yourself that you can be.

This book is just the beginning. It's the first in a series of books that will show you what successful people do in social media. Subsequent books will focus on specific social media platforms, such as LinkedIn, Twitter, and Instagram. Others will focus on life and career stages from high school through encore careers, and on groups from corporate leaders to entrepreneurs.

Let's get started!

Actions and Ideas

At the end of each chapter will be a summary list of actions and ideas you can consider as you build your social media savvy and boost you career. All of them are available in an accompanying free workbook called *Your Social Media Success Roadmap: 50 Questions, Actions and Ideas to Help You Boost Your Career.* It's available as a free PDF download at carolineleach.com.

CHAPTER 2

The 3 Big Trends Defining Careers of Today and Tomorrow

Before you dive into creating your social media strategy, it's valuable to take a step back and look at the bigger picture and the trends that will shape the future of work. These trends will help put your own career path into context. They'll also give you some additional anchors from which to start sharing content and building a network in social media.

With my corporate background in communications and marketing, I've studied the three big trends driving careers of today and tomorrow. During part of my tenure as vice president of Corporate Communications at DIRECTV, I had the good fortune to report to the Chief Human Resources Officer, Joe Bosch. Along with our CEO Mike White, Joe was a strong proponent of lifelong learning. They both advocated for and role modeled a relentless curiosity about everything that might affect our business.

Working with Joe gave me a good grounding in trend identification in two ways. The first was getting the assignment to create the company's inaugural, week-long leadership development program for the company's top executives, working with Joe and Mike. This was a stretch assignment. It built upon my existing skills while enabling me to pick up new skills in learning and development on the fly. It also exposed me to a variety of thinkers on leadership and how current trends impact management styles. It gave me a framework to apply strategy to any business challenge.

Mike taught a full day of strategy, based on his tenure as CEO of PepsiCo International and his leadership of DIRECTV. Jonathan Knee spoke on the changing media landscape, drawing from his book, *The Curse of the Mogul: What's Wrong with the World's Greatest Media Companies*. We had experts come in from Hogan Assessments, a top company in personality assessment and leadership development. We did experiential learning exercises that involved team challenges in the great outdoors. We were inspired by a visit from Paul Rusesabagina, the heroic hotel manager who saved more than 1,200 people during the Rwandan genocide. His story became the subject of the Academy Award-nominated film *Hotel Rwanda*. By working with these speakers and integrating everything I was exposed to in developing this program, I got a birds-eye view of the trends affecting leadership and the workplace.

The second way I learned to assess career trends was designing the annual leadership meeting for the company's top 200 people for nearly a decade, also working with Mike and Joe. Together we'd share ideas on the business plans and goals, the needs of our leaders, and the people who could bring important ideas to life on stage at the meeting.

The process involved talking about books and articles we'd read recently, TED talks we'd watched, and people we'd heard on podcasts and at conferences. Once we created a draft agenda and a potential lineup of speakers, we assessed our networks to figure out the best way to invite each one. Mike and Joe had created vast networks over the courses of their careers, so they often approached the speakers we identified, whether it was a direct ask or an indirect inquiry through others. In some cases we didn't know a speaker personally or anyone who might know that speaker. That's where the power of social media to connect with people often came in.

Our speakers opened a window into the future and helped me see patterns about what's ahead. Rita McGrath, the business strategy expert at Columbia University, talked about the end of competitive advantage based on her books about business strategy in an ever-changing world. Tony Schwartz, the CEO and the Founder of The Energy Project, presented about creating sustainable organizations for employees, based on his highly read New York Times article titled, "Why You Hate Work."[10] Ben Horowitz, the co-founder of the venture capital company Andreessen Horowitz, discussed the future of technology and innovation. Karie Willyerd, the chief learning officer at multiple Fortune 500 companies, talked about the workplace of the future and how to future-proof your career. These are just a few of the many profound and provocative thinkers I had the privilege of learning from firsthand in working with them as speakers and being part of the audience with my leadership peers.

During that time, I was also looking for speakers for the DIRECTV Women's Leadership Exchange, an employee resource group I led for a year as president. The starting point was making a list of distinguished female leaders in Southern California. One of them was Gwynne Shotwell. She's the president and chief operating officer of SpaceX, a private aerospace company that designs, manufactures, and launches advanced spacecraft and rockets. This company ultimately wants to make it possible for people to live on other planets, including Mars.

The only problem was I didn't know Gwynne personally. It wouldn't work to contact her directly. So I turned to LinkedIn to see if we had any connections in common. Luckily, there were seven. Of those, the one who seemed the most likely to have a strong relationship was a senior vice president on the DIRECTV engineering team, Phil Goswitz. I reached out to Phil, and he immediately agreed to send the invitation. Based on their working relationship, Gwynne said yes.

At our standing-room-only event, Gwynne talked about her career journey and the future of space exploration. It turned out to be the most well-attended meeting our group ever had. The power of professional networks and social media helped make it happen.

This is just one reason why it's so important to build your network, day by day and person by person. Chapter 6 will provide specific strategies on how to do this through social media.

Let's move into the three big trends that will affect your career. They are globalization, technology, and demographics. Together, they will have an unprecedented impact on the change we'll see in the workplace during our lifetimes.

Globalization Shrinks the World

We hear the term globalization a lot these days. But what does it mean and how does it impact the workplace, now and in the future?

Globalization is the "global integration of international trade, investment, information technology and cultures," according to Investopedia,[11] the New York-based website that covers investing and financial education and analysis.

According to the World Economic Forum, globalization has significant potential to increase innovation, productivity and growth throughout the world.[12] And the International Monetary Fund's World Economic Outlook noted that, "globalization—encompassing freer trade, increased foreign direct investment, and the international use of patents and copyrights—has substantially bolstered the diffusion of knowledge and technology."[13]

Increasingly, more companies are doing business in multiple countries. That steps up the level of skill and knowledge required of professionals to work with new technologies and to work cross culturally.

Another one of globalization's outcomes is that temporary positions are more common. More people are now becoming independent consultants, rather than full-time employees of large organizations. In fact, if the growth of freelancing continues on its current path, more than half of U.S. workers will be freelancing by 2027.[14]

This is the rise of what's often called the "gig economy." It refers to short-term assignments that people do as independent workers for various organizations. It can take the shape of specific projects where skilled people come together to complete a time-bound piece of work. It's similar to how groups of people convene to work on a motion picture and then go their separate ways once the film is complete.

In the corporate world, it's wise to act with the mindset of a consultant and bring the most value you can to your employer. This approach makes you a more valuable employee and prepares you to move more seamlessly among independent projects in the future. You can also start a side gig while holding down a full-time position, allowing you to test the market and your entrepreneurial capabilities.

The big caveat is that you must be sure to deliver the value and the work your employer expects. You have to honor the requirements to maintain the confidentiality of propriety company information. You must steer clear of perceived or actual conflicts of interest.

In parallel with all of this, author and corporate learning leader Karie Willyerd says, "everyone has dreams."[15] As Karie and her co-author Barbara Mistick wrote in their book *Stretch: How to Future-Proof Yourself for Tomorrow's Workplace*, finding meaning and purpose in your work helps you to be more engaged, productive and resilient.

My take on their view of the future is that a vibrant social media strategy lets you express your purpose and helps make your career dreams come true. Being active in social media can raise your profile among people who can open doors for you. That can be everything from the chance to work on a project to build your skills and your network, all the way to a promotion to your dream job.

The ever-evolving and increasingly temporary nature of work is at the center of what LinkedIn co-founder Reid Hoffman calls "tours of duty."[16] The term comes from the military, where it means a single assignment. It applies to the business world in focusing on a specific mission that has a well-defined end date.

Each tour of duty builds trust between the individual and the organization, and they may mutually agree to further tours of duty. Or they may decide to go their separate ways, with the person enriched by the skills and experiences they gained in the process. A tour of duty may also be one of the experiences that enables one to land their next tour.

As the size of the world shrinks through the growth of globalization, your ability to tell your story and build your network through social media will become increasingly important to your career success and your ability to navigate change.

Technology Connects Our World

Beyond globalization, technology is also changing everything about our lives, including our careers. There's artificial intelligence, augmented reality, virtual reality, robots, drones, bots, the internet of things, connected cities, cybersecurity, blockchain, bitcoin and so much more. Some of these terms and their implications may be familiar to you, and others may not. At times it feels like much more than the human brain and psyche can comfortably absorb. And much of technology makes our work more connected than it's ever been—both people to people and people to machine.

With this explosion in technology, it's estimated that more than half of all jobs could be automated within the next five years, according to the World Economic Forum.[17] Related to that, it's imperative to be constantly "reskilling" ourselves by seeking out new skills and experiences on a consistent basis to keep ourselves relevant and in demand. The Future of Jobs Report by the World Economic Forum underscores this need with the data point that, "the half-life of a skill has dropped from 30 years to an average of 6 years, and this holds true for even fresh university graduates."[18] Being a lifelong learner and consistently picking up new skills throughout the years has never been more important.

The technology fueling social media is a good example. Authors Guy Kawasaki and Peg Fitzpatrick say in their book *The Art of Social Media* that, "a 'social media guru' is an oxymoron, because nobody really knows how social media works."[19]

They go on to say, "No matter how smart you are, best practices always change, because the platforms change how their sites work. Therefore, everyone needs to keep experimenting."

An experimental mindset is what leads to new skills and innovative discoveries. Every year, for example, I do experiments in social media to see what I'll learn. The results provide interesting and unique insights for me to share on social media.

One year I blogged every day for a month. I learned that it's easier to do a specific activity on *most* days, rather than *every* day. I learned that to make a new habit stick, it's best to focus on just one new habit each month. I learned that the more effortless you make the process of achieving your goals, the easier it is to accomplish them. As an aside about making habits stick, these learnings came in handy in making meditation a regular practice in my life. By adding just one new activity during a specific month, I was able to make the habit become part of my daily routine.

Another year I posted content to LinkedIn every weekday for a month to test the data point that it takes about "20 LinkedIn posts every month to reach 60 percent of your audience."[20] What I learned is that posting daily increases the engagement with your network. Content that's shared by your network gets more engagement. And my experiment created unique, original content that ultimately attracted interest from my network. The data I collected and analyzed was my own, and therefore it was something only I could write about. As a result, people asked a lot of questions and invited me to speak at events so they could learn what would help their own social media activity.

This learning mindset didn't always come easily to me. A few years ago I was responsible for bringing social networking and social collaboration to employees at DIRECTV. At the time it was a new way of working in a social environment that enabled people to be more productive, collaborative, and innovative. It was my first real introduction to social media. Sure, I'd dabbled in Facebook in a personal sense. But the new project scared me.

Around that time, the actress, comedian, and writer Mindy Kaling appeared on the cover of Fast Company magazine, with the all-caps headline blaring, "Social Media is Sexy! (kinda)."[21] I felt like it was silently mocking me for everything I was *not*. I didn't believe I had the right experience. I wanted to crawl under my desk and hide until the social media project went away.

But that didn't happen, so I had to conquer my fear and move forward. As we were about to launch a pilot program, I decided I should start a blog. It would be available internally to fellow employees at the company. In this way, I could learn and be a role model for what it was like to try new things, potentially look silly in the process, and learn from everyone in the pilot community.

Ultimately, I knew I'd need to advise our C-Suite leaders on how to blog effectively to achieve their business goals and engage more fully with their teams. In order to do that, I needed to experience what it was like to blog for myself.

Through my willingness to take a leap, I discovered I loved the experience of blogging. I enjoyed bringing disparate ideas together, sharing my perspectives, and engaging broadly with employees throughout the company. I wrote about a range of workplace topics, with headlines like," "Five Ways to Inspire Innovation with Social Media," "Writing Irresistible Emails," and "Can Watching TV Help You Thrive on Change?" I enjoyed interacting with people's comments, fostering a dialogue, and helping connect people who were separated by their physical location and organizational structure.

Without pushing myself beyond my comfort zone and being willing to make mistakes in a public way, I wouldn't have built a new skill. I wouldn't have discovered a new path for myself. I wouldn't have been the role model that may have helped others.

Demographics Shape Our World

Demographics—the data about the population as well as groups within it—are changing. One of the biggest changes is the lengthening of our lifespans. Actuarial tables are now going up to 120 years, The Wall Street Journal reported.[22] More than half of babies born in developed nations in the 2000s can expect to live to 100 or beyond, says the medical journal The Lancet.[23]

People born before that will likely live a lot longer than they think. Many of us will be able to enjoy longer careers that change and evolve as we do and as the world does. This brings benefits as well as challenges as we navigate the new terrain of our lives.

Two researchers from the London Business School, Lynda Gratton and Andrew Scott, wrote a book called *The 100-Year Life: Living and Working in an Age of Longevity*. An asset they cited that's "key to a long and productive life" is your reputation.[24]

These authors say that, "a good reputation enables your valuable stock of skills and knowledge to be used in a productive way." A strong reputation enables you to expand your horizons and make many transitions that will happen over a longer lifespan.

"Social media will increasingly broadcast your image and value to others and allow others to monitor and track performance," they say. "So it's inevitable that you'll need to curate a brand and reputation that covers far more than just your professional behavior."

The Institute for the Future, a think tank based in Palo Alto, California, also underscores the importance of your reputation. In a brief on future skills, the "art and science of reputation management" is the top one.[25] "In the future," the report says, "you'll have to make yourself known in a 'digiverse' of billions of people. You will need to build your own personal brand for your own personal economy."

A personal brand is synonymous with your reputation. It's who you are, what you stand for, and how you add value to the world. Just as a product has a brand, so do you. Chapter 4 will delve into the concept of personal branding and how to build a powerful one for yourself.

The combination of globalization and technology accelerating the pace of change in the world, coupled with longer lifespans, also increase the need to continually refresh our knowledge. We must keep learning every day.

The Pulitzer Prize-winning author Thomas Friedman put it well in his book *Thank You for Being Late: An Optimist's Guide to Thriving in The Age of Accelerations*. He said, "Today's American dream is now more of a journey than a fixed destination—and one that increasingly feels like walking *up* a *down* escalator. You have to walk faster than the escalator, meaning you need to work harder, regularly reinvent yourself and engage in lifelong learning."[26]

One way we can learn every day is by tapping into social media. It helps us do this in three ways. First is by continually improving your social media strategies as the platforms and algorithms continue to evolve. You have to keep changing your approach as new features and networks are introduced, along with new ways people find to use them. Second is by tapping into social media to learn about any topic you choose. You can set alerts for areas of interest and go deep in learning about anything you want. Third is by sharing your new knowledge with your network and learning from their feedback by way of their comments and how they react to what you share.

The final aspect about demographics is that younger generations prefer to communicate digitally, often through social media and messaging apps, rather than in person. This includes Millennials, born from about 1980 to the mid 1990s, and Generation Z, born from about the mid-to-late 1990s on.

Since these two generations now account for more than half the U.S. workforce, being adept in communicating through social media makes everyone in the workplace better able to communicate, collaborate, and lead into the future.

Change is the defining characteristic of our lives and our worlds today and into the future. Globalization, technology, and demographics are combining to drive unprecedented change in how we work and how we live.

While constant change can be unsettling, embracing it is the key to successful future. Being curious about the world, being eager to learn, and being open to vulnerability are all important mindsets. They are also the hallmarks of what will help you to be successful in social media. But before you can do that, you have to be clear on who you are and how you show up in the world. The place to start is with getting the professional and personal blend right in social media, the subject of the next chapter.

Actions and Ideas

When thinking about the future and how globalization, technology, and demographics are likely to impact your career, consider the following:

How do you believe globalization will impact your field and industry? Could the work that you do be moved to another part of the world? How do you feel about the gig economy? Do you want to explore a side gig? How could you do that while you continue your day job?

What do you think technology will change about the work

that you do? Could some of it be automated? Are there areas that rely more on skills that are less likely to be automated, such as creativity, empathy, and critical thinking? How might you shift your work activities towards those to enhance your skills?

How long do you think you might live? How long do you *want* to live? How many different jobs or careers might you want to have? What topics do you want to learn about and how will you tap into social media to do that? What bigger purpose or meaning motivates you as the common thread running through your career and your life?

CHAPTER 3

Get the Personal and Professional Blend Right

D o you ever wonder how to keep your professional and personal social media activity separate and distinct? The answer is that you don't separate them. The reason is because you *can't* effectively keep them apart in today's world.

The way we live our lives now is all one big blend. What's personal is professional, and vice versa. The corollary is why there's no such thing as work-life balance, as much as we might wish there was. It's simply a work-life *blend*, where everything mixes together.

It's no longer possible or even desirable to try to separate parts of our lives into different spheres. Given the three big trends covered in Chapter 2 that shape our careers—globalization, technology, and demographics—the lines between different facets of our lives have blurred or been obliterated entirely. They are all one.

In my own life, I used to draw a dividing line. I tried to limit Facebook to friends and family. If a work colleague sent me a friend request, I invited them to connect on LinkedIn instead.

The people who defied categorization challenged my

framework. A work colleague, Elaine, was also involved with our school district's education foundation. Our paths often crossed at the office and at community events. Was Elaine a professional or a personal contact? In reality, she was both.

A similar principle applies to the content I share on social media. Some content might of interest to both my professional *and* personal networks. As an avid reader, I'm often asked about what I'm reading by colleagues and friends. Rather than feeling like I'm spamming people with article links in emails or texts, I share content I find interesting on Twitter. Anyone can opt in if they want by following me.

When posting to my blog about how professionals can build their careers through social media, I also share the content as a LinkedIn article. When LinkedIn prompts me to share the article via Twitter and Facebook, I always tweet about it. Less often, I share it on Facebook, due to the more personal nature of my network there.

When I launched my new company, though, I made an exception. Although it was largely business news for my professional network, I realized my personal network might be interested in the news too. Judging from the number of likes and comments, I was correct. In addition, my Facebook friend universe has grown to include more professional contacts over time, as the lines between the personal and professional continue to blur.

My strategy for Facebook friends has evolved to accepting friend requests generally from people I know, whether in the professional or personal realm. Given my recent role as a VP in the corporate world, I hang back on sending invitations to people in that space who might feel obligated to accept my request. I'm happy to connect if someone else invites me first, but I don't want to make colleagues feel awkward or uncomfortable about potentially declining a request from me.

Two university professors brilliantly addressed the concept of separating the personal and professional on social media in a Harvard Business Review article.[27] Ariane Ollier-Malaterre at the University of Quebec in Montreal and Nancy Rothbard at the Wharton School of the University of Pennsylvania researched how professionals use social media. They noted that many "felt compelled to accept friend requests from professional contacts." (This is the data-driven reason why I often steer clear of inviting professional colleagues to become Facebook friends). From their work, they identified four potential social media strategies.

The first is an open strategy. You post whatever comes to mind. There are no filters. Not surprisingly, this is a high-risk strategy and is not advised.

The second is an audience strategy. You keep your networks separate, as I used to do with friends and family in Facebook and work colleagues in LinkedIn. This makes sense for a while. But it increasingly becomes impossible to maintain as networks—and lives—become more fluid.

The third is a custom strategy. You post content to two different audience lists and/or on different accounts on the same platform. However, unless you have a lot of time on your hands or hire someone to manage your social media, this isn't a sustainable strategy.

The fourth is a content strategy. You post content that is mostly appropriate for all audiences, similar to a PG-rated film. In our increasingly blended world, this is an ideal strategy. You're consistent and efficient in how you connect across the personal and professional.

The authors recommend the custom or content strategies. While the custom strategy sounds good in theory, it's far too cumbersome for real life, with the time constraints we all face. You could certainly give it a try. My bet, though, is that you'll end up with the much more practical content strategy.

You can make your life simpler and more satisfying with the content strategy. "Everyone can see everything, so post appropriately for everyone," advises Allyson Rener, president of Murphy O'Brien, a public relations and digital agency focusing on luxury lifestyle, travel, and real estate. Taking this approach requires acting consistently and authentically in all that you do. Combined with a professional mindset, these are the qualities that will inspire trust in your networks.

"When you're on social media, you can't compartmentalize," says Heather Rim, the chief marketing and communications officer at AECOM, a global infrastructure firm based in Los Angeles.[28] "While I'm a fan of using a mix of platforms to tell your story, it's important to remember that it all ladders up to the one brand that is you."

Since it's impossible to separate the professional from the personal, what do you do if you want to vent or share something snarky in social media? You have two options, if your professional and personal reputation is important to you.

The first option is something we probably all heard from our parents or teachers—if you don't have something nice to say, don't say anything at all. The second option is to keep it to real life, in a face-to-face setting.

While authenticity is what will connect you the most with people in social media, it's important to couple it with professionalism. People are watching what you say and do in social media. How you present yourself will have a positive or negative impact on your career. You have to build credibility with a track record of delivering results. Your ability to consistently deliver results combined with authenticity about who you are will make for a winning combination on social media.

Behave in a way that will reflect positively on you and your company. A key way to do that is through original content you create and share in social media, which Chapter 7 will cover in detail. In addition, there are two other critical tactics—to look before you link and look before you "like."

Look Before You Link

It's important to be thoughtful not only about the content you post, but also about the content you share. The aggregate of what you share reflects on you just as much as original content you create and post. This compilation is known as curating content from a variety of sources that may be of interest to your network. Choosing carefully and wisely about what you share is part of what it means to act with social savvy in our rapidly changing world.

Nearly 60% of links shared in social media haven't been read first, according to The Washington Post.[29] If you care about your professional reputation, don't share links you haven't read in full. Take the time to review the content of *every* link you share in social media.

Sharing content implies that you endorse it and agree with it. Think of it like recommending someone for a job —your reputation is on the line. What if there's something lurking in that content link that *doesn't* represent your views? How will you know if you don't read it first?

When I worked at DIRECTV, I didn't share content that bashed the practice of watching television or the pay-TV industry. Often I'd find a great article on productivity, only to read it and discover that one of the suggestions was to watch less TV. Since that was in direct conflict with my employer's mission, I didn't share those articles. I also believe there are other productivity tips that are more effective and that TV enriches people's lives in a variety of ways.

Here are some guidelines to assess whether to share a particular link. Share links that aptly illustrate the topics you and your social media communities are interested in. Share links that provide relevant and appropriate data and metrics to support key points you want to make. Share links that position your company and its leaders in a positive and accurate light.

Here are examples of links that shouldn't be shared. Don't share links that have disparaging information about your company or its products. Don't share links that overly focus on your employer's competitors. Don't share links that cover topics you don't want you good name associated with—whether it's negativity, gambling, barhopping or other questionable topics. And don't share links with content that could be perceived as offensive or disparaging to any group or groups of people. If you're not sure, don't share it.

Always ask yourself if what you're sharing reflects positively on you, your employer, your family, and your community, before you post. If not, don't post it.

Here's a good tip from consultant and former Google executive Bill Duane that was covered in The New York Times about mindful moments. "Before posting anything on social media, ask yourself three questions," he recommends. "Is it true? Is it kind? Is it necessary?"[30] If it doesn't meet all three criteria, don't share it.

When you do find content to share that passes all of these tests, add your perspective. Briefly say what's important about it. Include a key takeaway or a memorable quote. Above all else, though, be sure you look before you link.

Look Before You Like

In addition to links you share in social media, have you thought about what all of your "likes" in social media say about you? More importantly, what do you *want* them to say about you?

Do you think before you "like" in Facebook and LinkedIn or "heart" in Instagram and Twitter? Do you consider how those pieces of data will be aggregated with thousands of other data points about you? Do you decide if it will reflect well on you or not? Just as you should look before you link, you should look before you "like."

The reason is because of what's called The Reputation Economy, covered in Chapter 1. In his book of the same name, Reputation.com founder Michael Fertik tells you "how to optimize your digital footprint in a world where your reputation is your most valuable asset."[31]

Ultimately, Fertik sets forth a compelling case that your digital reputation may shape how you experience the world—for better or for worse. Decisions may be made about you as a consumer—such as whether to extend credit or offer insurance and at what price—and as an employee—such as whether to interview you for a job opening or consider you for a promotion or a raise.

In recent years, for example, you may have wanted to be circumspect about your political views for privacy purposes and to keep the peace at your home or office. But your political leanings may have been identified, based on your social media activity. On Facebook, for example, you can see in your settings how the social network has identified your political views. Sure, there are privacy settings and rules about who sees your data, but it's not clear who may or may not have access to that information about you. I operate on the assumption that nothing is truly private.

You might want to think twice about what you "like" in the future. Here are my rules for liking content in social media. Always consider how liking something will reflect on you. Will it contribute to—or detract from—what you want to be known for? If you're not sure what certain content could imply, find out or don't like it.

If you have "friends" who repeatedly post content that seems strange to you, it might time to mute or unfriend them. While it's wise to expose ourselves to a variety of content and viewpoints so we can better understand the world, it doesn't mean that we have to subject ourselves to content that's overly offensive or demeaning.

Our friends and connections in social media and in real life reflect our values for others to see. Give careful thought to who you want to associate with. Ultimately, the quality of the people in your networks is more important than the quantity.

You have one life. Although it's made up of many facets, there is only one brand called YOU. Remember that *everything* you do on social media reflects on you in one way or another. Be clear on the story you want your activity to tell about you and act accordingly. To help you do that, we'll turn to how you can create a compelling and authentic personal brand in the next chapter.

Actions and Ideas

Here are some questions to ask yourself as you decide the best way to get the personal and professional blend right in social media:

How much do you like to compartmentalize the professional and the personal in your life?

Are you comfortable with everyone in your professional network seeing content you share with your personal networks and vice versa?

How much time do you have to devote to social media content creation? If your time is limited, you may want to strongly consider sharing content that is appropriate for everyone.

Do you read links fully before you share them in social media? Do you ensure you fully agree with the content and that it reflects well on you and your employer?

Do you think carefully before you "like" content, making sure it's aligned with your values and reflects well on you and your employer?

CHAPTER 4

Decide Who You Want to Be with a Compelling Personal Brand

W hat do you want to be known for in your career? What do you want people to say about your life? These are the questions that essentially answer the question, what is your personal brand?

A personal brand is a powerful strategy to communicate your unique value, in a way that feels authentic to you. Articulating your brand lets you take control of your career narrative and its trajectory. Having an intentionally created personal brand opens more doors to opportunity and accelerates your career progress.

Anyone and everyone has a personal brand, whether or not they consciously choose it and whether or not they are in the paid workforce. For example, a corporate manager, a stay-at-home parent, and a weekend musician all have a personal brand. The concept isn't limited to those in a professional role.

The revered management thinker and writer Tom Peters launched the concept more than two decades ago in a Fast Company article, The Brand Called You.[32] "Regardless of age, regardless of position, regardless of the business we happen to be in," he wrote, "all of us need to understand the importance of branding. We are CEOs of our own companies: Me Inc. To be in business today, our most important job is to be head marketer for the brand called You."

As the pace of change in the world has accelerated in the intervening two decades, a personal brand is more important than ever. Amazon founder Jeff Bezos is famously known for saying that a personal brand is "what people say about you when you're not in the room."[33]

What *do* people say about you? What do you *want* them to say about you? Are the answers to these questions the same, or do you need to change how you show up in the world and how people view you?

One way to start finding out what people say is by asking to participate in a 360-degree feedback process at your company. In this assessment, people you work with such as your supervisor, your peers, your direct reports, and other colleagues give feedback about your leadership and performance. Although its purpose is not specifically to identify your personal brand, it's often possible to see patterns in people's responses that give you a better idea of how you are perceived.

If you've completed a 360-degree assessment recently, you can also pull it out to see what you can take away from the aggregated data. The comments in particular are a rich resource to identify trends and themes in people's responses. Try not to get hung up on a single comment. But if you keep seeing the same feedback repeatedly, that's a strong signal about how you are viewed by many people.

You can also see how your public reputation stacks up through a Google search of your name. You should browse privately in the incognito mode, in addition to logging out of Google first. This will give you the best view of what others see when they Google your name, without the search results being influenced by your recent browsing history.

Search with your first and last name, along with any common misspellings of your name. You can also add your current employer after your name to see what comes up. Pay particular attention to what appears on the first screen, along with at least the next four screens. This is what people will likely see if they're searching for you as a potential job candidate, or even as a consultant or a speaker.

Ideally, your name should dominate the first page of a Google search, with positive content that reflects well on you. Maintaining current and active social media accounts with LinkedIn, Twitter, Instagram, and Facebook will help. A blog that you host on your own website can also help.

Over time, as you become more deliberate about the content you share in social media, your Google search results should improve. This is especially important if you have a common name that makes it more difficult to stand out in a search.

What if negative information comes up in a search? If it's incorrect, you could try working with the source to see if they'll correct the record. Beyond that, the best strategy is to continuously share new content on social media that presents you in a positive light as the professional you are. Over time the negative content should become less and less prominent.

One of the most fun things in life is to create the person you want to be. Author Steve Chandler who wrote the book *Reinventing Yourself* says, "You can be anyone you want. You invent yourself as you go. So be authentic and true to yourself."[34]

Someone I used to work with wisely said, "Be who you aspire to be right now." There's no need to wait. You don't have to "fake it until you make it." Just start taking action as the person you want to be today.

What Three Words Best Describe You?

Marketing strategy consultant, professional speaker, and author Dorie Clark says a personal brand really means your reputation. "Do people think of you as a person of integrity?" she asks in a conversation with Forbes contributor Kevin Kruse.[35] "Do they think your work is of high quality?"

To find out, she suggests asking a few friends and colleagues to give you three words that best describe you. You could even crowd source your answer in social media. Your LinkedIn network could be a great place to start.

In fact, I did something similar when I left the corporate world to start my own business. Colleagues sent me farewell emails that I found to be quite touching, to say the least. As part of naming my new business, I put all the descriptive words about me from those farewell notes into a spreadsheet. I was hoping the patterns and themes that resulted might help me come up with an ideal name.

Next I turned the spreadsheet into a word cloud so I could better see which words were the most prominent.[36] What came up? Some of the words that jumped out were leadership, social media, communications, learning, impact, inspiration, encouraging, positive, role model, LinkedIn, and Twitter.

Thankfully, these words all dovetail into my own personal brand statement. I love to help people and organizations tell their stories and embrace the future. I blog about how people can build their careers and companies through social media. It was reaffirming to see the words about who I am and what I do in the word cloud of how others see me.

I encourage you to try it for yourself. Your personal brand statement should combine the best of who you are and what you do with how you help other people. Then see if the personal brand you've developed is generally the same as how others see you. If the two are aligned and similar, congratulations to you. Keep up the good work. If they aren't as similar as you expected, you can take steps through the content you share in social media to create even closer alignment between how you see yourself and how others see you.

A Personal Brand is Especially Important for Women

A personal brand can be especially powerful for women. It could put you on the radar for exciting career opportunities, Dorie Clark writes in Harvard Business Review.[37] In the article, Dorie cites author and researcher Sylva Ann Hewlett, who says a personal brand is one of the best ways to attract a sponsor—someone who will champion you when you're not in the room and career decisions are being made.

Savvy use of social media may be able to help women overcome some of the unique challenges of working while female, the article goes on to say. There's the likability conundrum—where women are penalized when they violate gender norms to be likeable, agreeable, and modest. There's overcoming and neutralizing gender stereotypes and unconscious biases against women in leadership roles. And there's the fact that women are often promoted based on past performance, while men more often are promoted based on their potential. Consistently sharing high-quality professional content on social networks such as LinkedIn and Twitter can help women be perceived as having greater potential.

The upside of social media for senior-level women was quantified in a report by BRANDfog, a social media and digital reputation consulting firm for C-Suite leaders.[38] This includes C-level executives—people who have the word "Chief" in their title, such as Chief Executive Officer, Chief Financial Officer, or Chief Communications Officer. In a survey called The Power of Social Media for Women Executives, 96% of respondents agreed that women executives can use social media to build credibility and establish thought leadership. More than 90% agreed that women executives can use social media to build reputations to make them attractive candidates for the C-Suite. And 87% agreed that social media is an effective tool to promote equality among executives and in the C-Suite.

Just as women leaders benefit from a personal brand that they articulate on social media, men can build their careers as well by demonstrating their personal brand through the content they share over time.

The Power of Your Personal Brand

It's never too early in your career to think about and define your personal brand. In fact, it could even start in high school. At an annual service event at the University of Southern California, personal branding for high-school students was the focus of an intensive half-day experience.[39] The USC Annenberg School for Communication and Journalism paired students with alums to develop a personal brand statement.

Students thought about how they wanted to contribute to the world during their lifetimes and how that played into a personal vision statement. They also heard from alums and friends of the school about the power of a personal brand. Joining as an alumni leader and volunteer, I picked up new insights from students and alums alike about how to open doors with a strong personal brand.

What inspired me the most was the number of high-school students who have already started their own businesses. They gave social media tips for how they market themselves and their companies. An Instagram influencer with a large following shared what she learned from working with various brands and how to maintain her authenticity with her followers. A provider of babysitting services talked about marketing her business on Facebook, because that's where her mother's friends— her potential clients—are on social media. Yet another high-school student, a maker of children's toys, talked about his plans to scale his business more broadly, and how he's reached people through social media.

Veteran news reporter Al Naipo kicked off the event's speakers. After many years as a bureau chief, news reporter, and anchor with FOX 11 news in Los Angeles, he launched his own business and he led communications for Los Angeles County Supervisor Mark Ridley-Thomas. Al is now the Chief Administrative Officer at the Los Angeles Memorial Coliseum Commission.

Al focused on how to maintain professionalism with your personal brand when you're in the spotlight— whether it's politics, business, education, or any arena of life. He started by sharing a newsroom phenomenon—a large display listing reporters' social media followings, and how everyone ranks compared with their colleagues as well as competitor newsrooms. A social media presence is critical for journalists to be effective today. By extension, the same could be said for all professionals.

Al talked about the career opportunities that had come to him based on the strength of his LinkedIn profile, and he offered five nuggets of advice. First, your social media presence could be a make-or-break reason you get a job. Second, everything has to do with branding and how you're seen by others. Third, people view your work life and your personal life as all one thing. Fourth, stick with your brand because people associate it with you. And fifth, social media is a powerful way to connect directly with almost anyone.

What if you're more of a private person? How can a personal brand help you? Ashley Tesoriero, a national marketing specialist at IMT Residential, a multi-family residential investment and property management firm, told the group the secrets to sharing your personal story, even if you see yourself as a more private person. She emphasized the importance of tying your personal and professional life together to make one.

According to Ashley, your personal brand is, "your online and in-person resume you present to the world." She encouraged everyone to figure out what their story is, and what mediums best capture it. For her, it's Instagram, LinkedIn, and her WordPress website.

How do you get to your story? It starts with reflecting on your mission, vision and values. Ashley led the students through an exercise to begin thinking about these big-picture questions of what they want their lives to be about. The group outlined their personal experiences—complete with challenges, opportunities and who they are in their communities—in order to establish their personal brands. Reflecting on your own mission, vision and values can help lead you toward you own personal brand.

You can also create a "one-minute me" pitch. Emma Forbes, a radio and television presenter from the United Kingdom, shared how these work. A "one-minute me" tells your story. When doing this, Emma cautioned *not* to read a list of qualifications. Instead, she advised, "talk about where you come from, where you're going, and what you'd like to do."

She calls these the defining moments that happen in a face-to-face setting at pivotal moments in everyone's careers. What you put into your pitch also focuses your social media content. "You need to be the face of your brand," she said. "No one can sell it better than you. Be you and speak your view."

What do you do when nerves get the best of you? Emma gave some great tips. Start with deep breathing. Make eye contact. Pause instead of saying, "um." Clasp your hands in front of you.

Nerves aren't always a bad thing. "You *need* nerves," according to Emma. Then an emotional, electrifying moment arrived. She asked what would have happened, "if I wasn't nervous about meeting you today?"

If someone so accomplished, so authentic, and so poised felt nervous about speaking to students and alums, then there is hope for all of us. Bring on the nerves!

For anyone who wants to improve their public speaking skills, Toastmasters International is a great resource. Many meetings are held on corporate campuses, making it easy to fit into busy schedules. I remember my first introduction to Toastmasters early in my corporate career. One member had the role of "um" counter for each speaker. Another member served as the timekeeper. Everyone was invited to give feedback. It was truly a supportive and encouraging environment in which to practice, learn, and improve as a speaker.

On social media you also get the benefit of being able to craft and edit your words. Take that little bit of extra time to present yourself in a way that's true to your personal brand.

Kevin M. Yates, a self-described Learning & Development detective who solves mysteries just like Sherlock Holmes, emphasizes the importance of your personal brand. It comes through in everything he does in social media, including the background photo of a detective in his LinkedIn profile and highlighting the mystery he solves as, "did my training work?" He goes on to state that he measures impact and results for training and learning with facts, evidence and data.

"My personal brand message is facts, evidence and data for Learning & Development," he says, "so my social media posts, likes, shares, curations, and comments are mostly for content and topics that support my personal brand message."

Kevin further advises that, "jacks-of-all trades won't work on social media. Know your brand, know your message, and stay on it. Social media is valuable currency. Spend it wisely by staying on message and you'll be successful."

People who have strong personal brands lead with themselves and the unique value they contribute to the world. They don't define themselves by their current job title or the company where they currently work. Of course, it's important to be a good brand ambassador for your employer. But even more important is actively managing your own career through the power of your personal brand.

Follow Your Company's Social Media Policy

As you share your personal brand on social media, it's imperative to follow your employer's social media policy, in both the letter and the spirit. Be sure to read it, make sure you understand it, and apply it to how you show up in social media.

Most policies require you to disclose your affiliation with the company and make a statement in your social media profiles that the opinions you share are your own. Employers generally require that employees post in good taste and with respect for all groups of people.

Never, ever share the company's confidential, proprietary or sensitive information on social media. When in doubt about any content you want to share, ask your supervisor or other leader for guidance.

If you're at all on the fence about whether or not specific content is appropriate to share, don't post it. The mantra that it's better to be safe than sorry applies in spades here.

Above All Else is Your Authenticity

Beyond staying on the right side of your company policy, what's most important about your personal brand is authenticity. Be yourself and be the best you that you can be.

"You are your own competitive advantage," says Carla Harris, a leader with a fascinating life as a Morgan Stanley executive, a gospel singer, and a bestselling author. "The last thing you should ever do is submerge that which is uniquely you," she says in a leadership talk at Arizona State University where she shares her pearls of wisdom about her career and her life.[40]

The underlying reason has to do with confidence, Harris believes. "As quiet as it is kept, most people are not comfortable in their own skin," she says, "so when they see someone who is comfortable and confident in their own skin, they will gravitate towards that. They *want* some of that."

Carla's life could fit the definition of a multi-hyphenate, or someone who does several different jobs. This term is especially common in the entertainment industry, where a celebrity might be referred to as a singer-actor-producer-writer-entrepreneur. How does Carla's life as a banker-singer-writer square with Kevin Yates' advice for a laser-like and singular focus in social media?

As with many aspects of life, it depends on situation. Carla found that when her banking clients got wind of her gospel singing on the side, it made her a more interesting person to them. It helped her to stand out. It made her more authentic.

A former colleague of mine, Earl Bonovich, who received an Emmy Award for his work on sports event coverage, sums it up well. "One of the most successful things in social media is remaining true to yourself," he says, "which allows you to truly connect with others."

Perhaps the case for authenticity is best expressed in the timeless words of the Greek philosopher, Socrates. He is credited with saying, "the way to gain a good reputation is to endeavor to be what you desire to appear."

◆ ◆ ◆

Actions and Ideas

As you create your personal brand, here are some questions to get you started:

Do you know how others perceive you? Try asking key people in your professional circle to share a few words about how they view you. Look for patterns and themes in the responses.

What are your biggest dreams for what you want to accomplish in your career and your life? Then think about how you *want* to be perceived by others for the value you bring to the workplace. How does this relate to how others see you? Do you need to make some adjustments in your behavior to close any gap?

What is your personal brand statement in a sentence? What is it that you help people do so they can achieve their own goals? In my case, I love to help people and organizations tell their stories and embrace the future, enabling them to achieve their dreams and realize their potential.

Have you looked at your company's social media policy recently? Are you following it? Are you a good ambassador for your employer's brand and your own?

How authentic do you believe you are in social media and in real life? How could you be more authentic to who you truly are? Is your authenticity backed up by a demonstrated ability to achieve results?

CHAPTER 5

Pick Where to Play

Once you define what you want to be known for through defining your personal brand, you need to choose where you're going to tell your story. You need to select which social media networks to be active on and where to invest your time.

A good starting point is identifying what you want to accomplish with social media. Essentially, it's deciding what game you're playing so you can pick where to play.

Do you want to build your network? Join a special project to round out your skills? Become known as an expert in your field? Land a new job? Position yourself for a promotion? Change careers?

As I covered in Chapter 1, I did a study to learn how fellow professionals are using social media to build their careers. As part of it, I started with questions about why people are active in social media. Building a network, accessing news about an industry or profession, and learning continually about an industry or profession are the top three reasons.

Being clear on what you want to do on social media will make it easier to choose which networks to be on and how much time to devote to each of them. Remember that your goals will change and evolve as your career does and you do. For that reason, you'll want to remain flexible and continually assess and refine your approach.

Once you know what game you want to play, you can pick where you want to play. There are lots of platforms, but you don't have to engage on every one of them. Pick one to get started. And ultimately choose two or three where you'll invest the majority of your time.

The specific content you share in social media will be covered in Chapter 7. Don't think that you don't have anything to say because you're in the early stages of your career or you feel you haven't done anything noteworthy. You may have systems and processes and ways to solve problems that you take for granted but that could be helpful to others. I was fascinated to learn that David Allen, the bestselling author of *Getting Things Done* for time management, was simply documenting the systems he'd created for himself when he wrote his first book. He talked about it with Chandler Bolt in an episode of the Self Publishing School podcast.[41] David Allen's experience illustrates that what may seem mundane or routine to you could be incredibly valuable to others.

The main social networks to consider are your own blog, LinkedIn, Twitter, Instagram, Facebook, Snapchat, and YouTube. Let's take a look at the advantages of each one.

Own Your Content with a Blog on Your Own Website

If you want to establish yourself as a thought leader in your field, your own blog is the best way to do it as a start. If you've learned a lot in your career, a blog is great way to share your knowledge. If you have a unique or contrarian point of view in a professional area, a blog is an ideal way to convey your perspective.

The word "weblog" was first used in 1997. It referred to a series of internet posts in chronological order, similar to a diary or a journal. By 1999, the word was shorted to "blog," which we still use today, a few decades later.

With millions of blog posts now flooding the internet on a daily, weekly and monthly basis, there's a great deal of competition for attention. But your blog doesn't have to attract a huge following in order to help boost your career. It all depends on what goals you're trying to achieve with your blog. Are you trying to get hired into an entry-level job? Are you developing expertise in a new field to change careers? Are you positioning yourself as a senior-level thinker and leader?

As long as you can make your blog visible and accessible to the people you might need to influence in order to accomplish your goals, then you can consider it a success. That could mean a hiring manager, a mentor who can advise you on your career path, or a potential sponsor who will champion you in talent conversations that take place at your company.

The benefit to having your own website to host your blog is that you own your content, as long as you continue paying for the domain name and hosting costs. From a personal branding perspective, try to secure your first and last name as the domain for your website.

For example, my blog is at carolineleach.com. When I launched The Carrelle Company, I bought the domain name carrelle.com. Because the company is relatively new and I'm not at a point where I want to develop and maintain two separate websites, the carrelle.com website points to carolineleach.com, where I've expanded the content beyond the blog that was my starting point.

If your name is already taken as a domain name, but an active website doesn't seem to be in use, you could try to buy the domain from the person who owns it. Do a Google search to figure out the current ways to do that. If your name is taken and the website *is* active, try adding your middle initial to see if that version is available.

Once you have your blog domain name, then make your other social media handles as similar to each other as you can. For example, I use @caroline_leach for Instagram and Twitter and leachcaroline for LinkedIn and Facebook. This makes it simpler for people to find you and engage with you.

It also makes it easier for people to find your blog, and easier to own and protect your content. If you share your content solely on other social media platforms, you can't control what ultimately happens on that site. Although it's not likely, what if a site suddenly closed? What if it was sold to another company and your content was lost in the transition process? What if its algorithm suddenly changed and your connections weren't seeing your content to the same degree? You can sidestep any of these possibilities and more simply by establishing your own blog.

I chose WordPress because of its simplicity and ubiquity. WordPress is now estimated to run about 30% of the world's websites.[42] You can use it for your own personal website, including your blog. And there are many other options besides WordPress for hosting your blog and your website. A Google search will show you all the current ones as well as people's reviews on the pros and cons of each.

While some people could argue that a blog is not technically social media, others put it squarely in the social media camp because of its community-building element. Blogs are meant to spark comments and dialogue around your ideas, creating a community in the process.

Where the traditional social media networks come into play is in extending the reach of your blog to a bigger audience. How many blogs do you personally visit in the course of a day or a week? I'd guess not many. But how many articles do you read in your social media feeds via Twitter, Facebook, and LinkedIn? I'm guessing quite a few more.

Two years into my blog, I wasn't reaching a large audience. I loved writing it. I loved bringing ideas together in new ways. What I didn't love was promoting my content. The last thing I want to do is waste people's precious time by pestering them to read my latest blog post that might not be relevant to their life.

What I began to do a few years ago was to repurpose my blog content as LinkedIn articles and tweet the LinkedIn link. What made me start doing this? As I discussed in Chapter 2, it's part of my process to conduct experiments on social media from time to time to see what I'll learn from it. In testing the data point that, "it takes about 20 LinkedIn posts every month to reach 60% of your audience,"[43] I decided to post content to LinkedIn every weekday for a month.

As part of coming up with enough content, I decided to repurpose a blog post as a LinkedIn article every Wednesday. After just a few weeks, my articles began attracting more readers. People begin leaving comments and sharing my articles. Others started inviting me to speak to their groups about what I was learning in the process.

On occasion I've shared blog posts on Facebook, if the content could be something of interest to a more personal audience. For example, in my corporate farewell post about all the great people I worked with, it seemed like important news for my more personally oriented network too. But normally I don't repurpose my blog content on Facebook, because my friends there are more likely to be interested in my personal life and my family, rather than the details about my career.

If you're serious about being considered a thought leader in your field, a blog is the best place to start. You can build your community on a website that you own, and you can promote it and extend its reach through your social media accounts.

Build Your Network and Be a Thought Leader on LinkedIn

LinkedIn is the world's largest professional network, with a mission to "connect the world's professionals to make them more productive and successful."[44] It launched in 2003, and Microsoft bought it in 2016. Today it has nearly 600 million users as of this writing. More than 260 million people access it daily. Well over 90 percent of recruiters tap into LinkedIn to find candidates for open positions.[45]

LinkedIn is *the* place where every professional should be. It's the "North Star" for professionals, the number-one gathering spot, and the nexus for your network. You can develop a robust profile over time that tells the story of your career and where you're heading. You can actively build a broad and diverse network of everyone you know in business and everyone you want to get to know. You can share your professional expertise through posts and articles.

Increasingly, LinkedIn has become your real-time resume. It's a living expression that you can develop and grow throughout your career, as you add experiences, positions, projects, and more over time.

The ability to post articles is a perfect way to amplify the content on your blog and reach a bigger audience. As you grow the size of your network on LinkedIn, you can reach more people with your content. You also build a robust content repository that leaders in your company, job recruiters, and others can access to understand how you think and act in the business world. This in turn might open doors to new projects, new positions, and new opportunities.

Be a Thought Leader and Get Real-Time News on Twitter

Twitter is a news and social networking site that describes itself as, "what's happening in the world and what people are talking about right now."[46] About 330 million people use Twitter to send tweets, or status updates. Tweets used to be limited to 140 characters, but the length was expanded to 280 characters. Because of the relatively short length of a tweet, using Twitter is also known as "microblogging."

You can follow people of interest on Twitter. As of January 2019, Statista reports the most followed people on Twitter are Katy Perry (107 million followers), Justin Bieber (105 million), Barack Obama (104 million), Rihanna (89 million), and Taylor Swift (83 million).[47] Some of the top business leaders on Twitter include Tim Cook of Apple, Bill Gates of Microsoft, Mary Barra of GM, Elon Musk of Tesla and SpaceX, and Richard Branson of Virgin, to name but a few inspiring business leaders you could follow.

One of the reasons I joined Twitter was to share what I'm reading. As an avid reader of news, articles, blogs, and books, I'm often eager to share interesting tidbits of what I'm learning. But the last thing I want to do is be the person burdening my colleagues and friends with incessant emails about the latest article I read. So instead, I share in my Twitter feed some of the interesting things I have read. In addition, I use Twitter to share my blog posts and LinkedIn articles, to provide helpful information about social media marketing, and to amplify the work of organizations where I hold volunteer leadership roles.

My editor, Cat Spydell, uses Twitter to share articles she wants to keep a record of for future reference. Her Twitter stream serves as a personal database, as well as information she hopes those who follow her find interesting, too.

Another use for Twitter is live tweeting an event. When I'm at a conference, for example, I take pictures or videos of the speaker or panelists and listen for sound bites I can tweet. I use the most action-oriented and flattering pictures of people, along with the event hashtag so the content is more easily discoverable by those at the event or those who are following the event.

Brand Your Career Visually on Instagram

The vision of Instagram is to "capture the world's moments." It launched in 2010 and Facebook acquired it in 2012. It's a fast-growing social network with more than one billion monthly active users and 500 million active users of Stories—photos and videos that are only displayed for 24 hours.[48]

Because Instagram is such a visual medium, where beautiful eye-catching photos and videos are what attract followers, it has great potential as a visual brand builder for professionals. Its rapid growth means you can reach an increasingly broader audience. And its popularity among Millennials and Generation Z creates opportunities to connect with younger groups of people.

Launching my first social media research led to a volunteer leadership colleague Tom Henkenius introducing me to Tiffany Frake, the founder of the Sparkset app for career exploration. As part of her work, she created an Instagram account for the Sparkset app that follows hundreds of accounts with great examples of people showcasing their professional lives—from mobile product managers to spine surgeons and from corporate lawyers to graphic designers.

Increasingly, Instagram is a place to share visual representations of what you do on the job. It lets you bring a creative flair to your work life and express who you are and what you do to make a difference in the world. If your followers on Instagram are mainly family and friends, you can start with sharing glimpses of your work life, along with the usual content that you share. Perhaps you attended a conference that might be of interest to them, or you spoke at an event. As you weave elements of your professional pursuits into your Instagram feed and your Stories, you can assess how your network is— or isn't—responding, and you can adjust your approach accordingly.

Make Your Colleagues Your Friends on Facebook

Facebook launched in 2004 and now has 2.32 billion monthly active users.[49] Its mission is to "give people the power to build community and bring the world closer together." Facebook is transcending friends as people connect more and more with work colleagues, as I explored in Chapter 3 on getting the professional and personal blend right in social media.

Seemingly everyone is on Facebook, making it a good place to reach a lot of people. You can have your work colleagues become friends on Facebook and build stronger professional relationships by appropriately and judiciously sharing more of your personal life.

There are two aspects to keep in mind, however, as you think about Facebook as a way to boost your career as a professional. The first is that your network may be predominantly family and friends with a focus on your life outside of the office. Your Facebook friends may not be interested in the details of what's happening in your company or your industry. The second is that your time is limited and you need to focus your efforts. There are other social networks where the return on investment for your time is much higher.

For these reasons, it's a good idea to be mindful of the content you share on Facebook. It's likely being seen by people in your social circles as well as in your work world. If you have limited time to spend on social media for career building, as is the case for most busy professionals, then Facebook isn't necessarily where you need to focus the majority of your time. You can use it to selectively share work highlights that your family and friends might enjoy.

Experiment and Connect on Snapchat

Snapchat launched in 2012, with the ability to share disappearing photos. Its parent company, Snap, is in business to "contribute to human progress by empowering people to express themselves, live in the moment, learn about the world, and have fun together."

Snapchat is highly popular with Millennials, and even

more so with the younger Generation Z. Part of the appeal is that Snapchat is perfect for capturing all the less-than-perfect moments in all of our lives.

I joined Snapchat to connect with younger family and friends, have fun, and experience what used to be the fastest-growing social network. I was also curious about how businesses were using it to build their brands.

It felt at first like the feeling when I first joined Twitter. I wasn't quite sure what to do with it. I didn't fully know why I was there. I couldn't yet articulate what I wanted to accomplish. And that was okay. Part of learning why you're on a social network and how you can use it is to experiment and play with it.

Before Instagram introduced Stories in 2016, I viewed Snapchat as a place to experiment, stay current, and have fun. However, the advent of Stories on Instagram provides a great sandbox to experiment with ephemeral content and reach a large audience. As a result, Snapchat isn't a place where I spend a great deal of my social media time. But I must say, it's definitely still fun!

Embrace the Power of Video with YouTube

The first video was uploaded to YouTube in 2005, and Google bought YouTube in 2006. Its mission is to "give everyone a voice and show them the world." YouTube currently has 1.3 billion users. It gets 30 million visitors every day who watch 5 billion videos daily.

Video is how people prefer to consume content. By 2021, video is expected to account for 82% of all internet traffic, according to a Cisco study.[50] Starting your own video channel on YouTube could be a good option for you to create a series of "how to" videos relative to your professional work. It could also be very labor intensive. It's something you have to balance with all the other demands on your time.

One of my former colleagues, Angelica Kelly, created a successful "passion project" channel called You Brew Kombucha.[51] Fascinated by kombucha, a beverage produced by fermenting sweet tea with a culture of yeast and bacteria, Angelica filmed more than thirty "how to" videos over a single weekend. Her YouTube channel has attracted more than 23,000 subscribers, and it's still growing.

If you have an interest in video and a story to tell that lends itself to video, YouTube could be a great social network for you to boost your career.

Where Should You Play?

To sum it up, your best bets for social media to boost your career are a personal blog, LinkedIn, Twitter, and Instagram. Your blog is the home base and the anchor for your content and for you as a professional. LinkedIn is the long-term investment in your career, where you build your profile, your network, and your content consistently over time. Twitter and Instagram are for real-time sharing.

If you want or need to limit your involvement to two, pick a blog and LinkedIn. If you want to expand it to three, add Instagram. Why? Its fast-paced growth means you can reach more people and have more of an impact.

Keep in mind that social media platforms are always changing and evolving—both the features of the platforms such as their algorithms, as well as the platforms themselves. Remember how MySpace and Tumbler began as social networks? Remember the now-defunct Google+, Yik Yak, and Friendster?

It's important to keep an eye on how social networks are changing and evolving over time. When a new network comes on the scene, you might want to experiment and try it out. When a site seems to be losing steam, you might want to shift your limited time to other platforms.

With that said though, LinkedIn, Instagram, and Twitter are large enough that it's a relatively solid bet to focus on them for the foreseeable future.

Now that you've picked where you'll play in social media, it's time to build a network that will be the source of introductions, ideas, and inspiration.

Actions and Ideas

As you decide where to play in social media, here are some questions to consider:

What are your goals in social media? Do you want to build your network? Join a special project to round out your skills? Become known as an expert in your field? Land a new job? Position yourself for a promotion? Change careers?

Once you are clear on your goals, you can pick where you want to play in social media. Does your expertise or perspective lend itself to a blog? Could you experiment with posting a few articles on LinkedIn before you establish your own website to host your blog?

Are you on LinkedIn? Is your profile completely filled out and up to date?

Does Twitter make sense for you? If you're not already on it, consider creating a profile simply to get real-time news and observe what people are saying and doing on it.

Are you on Instagram? What are the highly visual elements of your work that lend themselves to this platform?

Do other networks such as Facebook, Snapchat, or YouTube make sense for what you do in your career?

CHAPTER 6

Build Your Network

Who you know and who knows you is becoming more and more important in our technology-driven world. Relationships with people are what will open doors to new projects, new jobs, and new careers. This web of relationships is what forms your professional network—a group of people who will help each other in their careers and share useful information and insights.

Your network consists of the various communities you build in real life and on social media. Your network is one of the biggest assets and advantages you can build over the course of your career. Jobs will come and go, but members of a network can help each other indefinitely.

There are two types of network members, called "bonding" and "bridging" capital from the work by Robert Putnam, a Harvard University sociologist.[52] Bonding capital means relationships that are built on what you have in common. These relationships probably represent the bulk of your network, because it's easy and comfortable to connect with people who are similar to you. Bridging capital means relationships that are made with people who are different from you. Having more bridging capital in your network enables you to tap into new and different ideas and networks of people. It may help you to think more innovatively and expansively. It may broaden your exposure to people in other industries. As you build your network over time, it's important to seek both bonding and bridging relationships.

Engaging with a community is more important than ever. Why? Social media algorithms are constantly changing. Organic reach—the content you don't pay for when you post—is declining. Having a community of committed people is important because they are the ones who will like, comment on, and share your content.

A committed community of followers is critical and makes your content all the more accessible and visible, in a virtuous cycle. That is one of the big reasons why having a community of committed people is so important. Having a deliberate plan for building a robust and diverse network is a career imperative.

Make LinkedIn Your Network Central

The best place to catalogue your network is on your LinkedIn account. Consider LinkedIn the foundation for all of your networking efforts. Because social media platforms can change at any time, make it a habit to download your contacts at least a few times a year into a separate file you keep. That way, if anything goes sideways with LinkedIn, you'll still have a relatively recent list of all your contacts.

To start expanding your network, assess its current state. Look at both the quantity, or the number of connections, and the quality, or the overall value of your connections. A smaller network of people who are more meaningfully related to you and your career is better than a bigger network that's a more random assortment of people you don't know well. Just keep in mind the importance of having a balance of "bonding" and "bridging" connections, regardless of the size of your network.

Start with the people in your contact list on your smartphone. Are you connected with all of them in LinkedIn? If not, LinkedIn has a feature that enables you to connect with all of them—or the ones you choose from your contacts list—simultaneously.

Whenever you send a LinkedIn invitation, it's a good idea to personalize it, rather than sending the default invitation. A personalized invitation makes you more memorable, increases the likelihood that your invitation will be accepted, and strengthens your relationship.

In addition, you can follow key members of your network on Twitter and Instagram, as well as friending them on Facebook. In the corporate world as a leader of other people, my personal rule was to invite members of my team to connect on LinkedIn. But I let them take the lead on other social networks—for example, if they sent me a Facebook friend request, I accepted, but I didn't initiate the invitation. My reason was to give people their personal space in social media, as I discussed in Chapter 3. I wanted to avoid putting them in an awkward position of potentially not wanting to accept my invitation but not wanting to offend me as a result.

The flip side of that is being able to connect with more senior leaders at your company as well as luminaries in your industry. You can always follow people of interest on Twitter and Instagram. And you can send a personalized LinkedIn invitation explaining why you'd like to connect. Take a look at any mutual connections first to see if you can identify any patterns in the connections, especially if there are connections who are similar to you in functional area and level. This makes you more visible to people who may be in a position to open doors for you.

As Richard Butler, a learning, design and technology leader who transforms research into results, says, "what's great about social media is that it allows everyone to have a seat at the proverbial table and partake in the 'feast' of information, insights, and inquiries." Pull up a chair and let the conversation begin.

In addition, assess the relative size of your bonding and bridging relationships. It's likely you may need to focus more on building bridging connections. Look beyond people who are similar to you to find people of different backgrounds, ages, career fields, and so on to develop new relationships.

Connect Every Day

Once you're connected with everyone you know, think about the people you will soon meet or want to get to know. You can scan your calendar each week to see if you'll be meeting anyone new. You can visit their LinkedIn profiles and other social platforms to get to know them in advance. You could send them a personalized LinkedIn invite before the meeting. When you meet in person, you'll already be acquainted with each other's LinkedIn profiles and you may find a great conversation starter. For example, maybe you know interesting people in common or your new connection may be working on a project you want to learn more about. Just keep it light and friendly, though, so no one feels like a cyberstalker has turned up too many personal details on them.

Give some thought to new activities you've gotten involved with. Did you join a new professional group? Are you on a community board? Participating in a mentoring circle? Anytime you join a new group, connect with the people in your preferred social channels, starting with LinkedIn.

When I attend conferences that share the attendance list, I send personalized invitations to the people who attended. If I get the list in advance of a meeting, I'll send invitations before we ever meet in person. That's often a good way to seed a vibrant conversation when we do meet. I'm able to see their interests, connections, schools, and other potential points of conversation starters.

One such invitation led to a speaking invitation. After attending a leadership conference, I sent personalized LinkedIn invitations to the people who attended. Kavita Gupta was one of them. She looked at my LinkedIn profile as a result and invited me to speak to a local chapter of the Association of Talent Development. We decided to meet in person over lunch and discovered we actually live in the same community. Were it not for social media, however, our paths might never have crossed.

When I read professional publications and articles, I sometimes send personalized invitations to the authors. I include a comment on a specific part of their piece that resonated with me, or a key takeaway I got and something I am doing differently as a result of reading their work.

When I listen to a great podcast, I sometimes send personalized invitations to the host and the guest. Usually I'll leave a review on iTunes first, sharing specifically how the content helped me. In my connection invitation, I'll mention my biggest takeaway from their content as well as that I posted a review of the podcast.

Any time I'm speaking at an event I make an effort to connect with the other speakers on social media. If I'm speaking on a panel with people I haven't met before, I'll connect on social media so we can get to know each virtually in advance of our panel discussion.

Social networks also recommend new connections. Take advantage of those. You don't necessarily need to connect with everyone on the list, but scroll through the recommendations a few times each year to see if there's anyone you'd like to add.

Make the most of serendipitous moments. At the airport recently, I ran into Tracey, someone I met a few years ago at an event at my son's school. We struck up a conversation and caught up on what was going on at our respective employers. To keep the connection going, I followed up with a LinkedIn invitation.

One of my professional associations is a roundtable for senior communicators and public relations leaders. When I attend a meeting, I send personalized invitations to my fellow leaders in attendance. One of the members has a good strategy—she sends LinkedIn invitations in real-time during roundtable discussions.

Give some thought to people you'd like to meet. Are you working in a new area and want to learn from luminaries in the field? Are there companies of interest you want to know more about? Are there second-level connections—contacts of contacts—you'd like to add to your network? This is where the personalized invitation is especially important. Explain in a compelling and brief way why you'd like to connect.

You could also look at alumni groups and people who have similar degrees. I picked up this idea from Lucas

Buck, an area sales manager at Farmers Insurance who spoke at a networking breakfast for my son's school. Lucas uses LinkedIn to achieve his business objectives and attract new talent to the insurance business. When he spoke at the group, I sent personalized LinkedIn invitations to everyone there, along with Lucas.

Create a Framework for Accepting Invitations

When your LinkedIn app fills up with connection invitations, what's your strategy for deciding yes or no? When someone sends you a friend request on Facebook, how do you decide whether or not to accept? If you create a general framework for which invitations you accept and which you don't, it will save you time and result in a better network of people you truly want to be connected with.

Some people recommend connecting only with people you know and trust. Others set a higher bar and recommend only connecting with people you'd be willing to ask a favor of or do a favor for. However, if someone takes the time to personalize a connection request with a well-articulated reason for wanting to connect, I will generally accept.

But what about the invitations with no personal note or the friend requests from people I don't know? A simple and efficient option is to simply delete them all. But you might miss some really great people as a result.

Here's my framework for which invitations I will automatically accept, without having to think through each one. I'm always happy to connect with people who are fellow colleagues at current or former employers. I'm glad to connect with people who work in the same industries as I've worked in, such as technology, media, and telecommunications. I'm open to connecting with people who belong to the same professional, community, or civic groups that I belong to. I'm glad to connect with people from my alma maters—whether they're students, alums, professors, or staff members. If someone attended a conference with me, I'm happy to connect. I'm also eager to connect with people who add to the diversity of my network on various dimensions, including industry, geography, career stage, functional area, and so on. This adds more bridging relationships to my network. There's also a wild card element for me. Someone with an interesting background who catches my attention is someone worth connecting with. It's hard to articulate this one, but I know it when I see it. I believe you will, too.

The next group of invitations is less clear cut. I will consider connecting with people who have mutual connections. This comes with a big caveat, however. An underlying rationale for the connections has to be evident to me. Recently I declined LinkedIn invitations from people who had a high number of mutual connections, but for which I couldn't discern a compelling reason *why* we were mutual connections. Usually it was because they didn't work in the same industry or even one that could be considered in some way related. I suspect that the person may be relying on "social proof," as a way of increasing their network with people they don't know personally. Because people are often pressed for time, if they see familiar people in their network who are connected with the requester, they may accept the invitation without further thought.

Lastly is the group of invitations that I will decline. These include people with no clear connection to any areas of my work. A lack of clarity about what the person or their company does is another red flag for me. Any suspicious-looking profiles, such as no last name listed or little information included in the profile is usually a decline. Anything that appears sales-related is also a decline. If I'm looking for a new vendor partner, I'll go to my trusted network first for recommendations, not to random connections on LinkedIn or Twitter.

Connect Your Connections the Right Way

One of the benefits of a robust network is being able to connect members of your network to each other who could benefit from knowing each other. It's fun and rewarding to act as a boundary spanner, connecting people across networks.

There's an etiquette to this process that will make the recipients of your introductions much more likely to participate and to retain goodwill toward you as a member of their network.

Often what you learned growing up will help you in the professional world. One of my mom's rules was if I wanted to invite a friend over, I had to ask my mom in private, without the friend being part of the conversation. Why? In case my mom needed to say no, it wouldn't create an awkward moment.

The same logic applies to introducing people in your network to each other. Ask each one, privately and separately, if it's okay to make the introduction. David Burkus, a bestselling author, refers to this practice as "permission introductions" in a great Harvard Business Review article called The Wrong Way to Introduce People Over Email.[53] The right way according to David is also called a "double opt-in introduction."

As you reach out individually to each person, give context and background for the request. Don't say you think the two should meet each other and put the burden on your contact to figure out why. No one has the time to do that, and it will strain your relationship with them. You could be seen as a person who isn't fully respectful of their time.

Share with each person *why* you think they'd benefit from knowing each other. Include your thoughts on how they might be able to help one another. Add a glowing fact or two about each person, so they have a place to start a conversation.

There are many reasons why I introduce people. The first is for career advice for people on my teams in the corporate world. There may be people in my network who can help others with a current work challenge, or to explore a future functional area of interest. At one time I led a marketing leadership development program in collaboration with colleagues in human resources, so I introduced interested employees to current participants in the program. They were able to learn about the program, meet a new colleague, and learn about another area of the company.

Sometimes I want to pay it forward. Many people provided information and advice to me early in my career as I was trying to make a change from a supply chain role into a corporate communications position. At the time, I didn't feel I had a lot to give back. But now I can help people early in their careers benefit from the people in my network. For a job shadow day with college students, I arranged a series of informational meetings with colleagues who shared their career paths and what they do in their current jobs.

Once you have the green light from each person, you can make an introduction via email. Include a compelling, complimentary and descriptive line or two about each person. Hyperlink to anything helpful or noteworthy about each person. Add why they'd benefit from meeting each other.

One of my former colleagues Anthony Robbins is especially good at this. When we worked at the same company, we only met virtually through social media. But we scheduled a call to see how we could help each other in our work. He was highly gifted at seeing who in his network could benefit from meeting each other, and explaining his thought process in brief introductory messages.

Make the immediate next step easy and clear. The more junior person—generally the one gaining the most from the introduction—should take the next step of finding a time on the other person's calendar, without creating extra work for that person.

Be kind to your network by not suggesting *too* many introductions in a short period of time. Space them out by at least a few months. If there's more than one introduction you want to make to the same person, prioritize the most important one first.

And some introductions should never be made. You don't want to waste the time of people in your network or take advantage of their goodwill. Your credibility and reputation will suffer as a result. Don't introduce a job candidate without at least a 70% match with the job description to the hiring manager. Don't introduce a salesperson you don't know well to business decision makers in your network.

Don't introduce anyone who isn't clear about why

they're requesting to be introduced to someone in your network. For all you know, they may be putting someone in an awkward position who is a valued member of your network. How is that person going to feel about you?

Given the importance of reciprocity, be open to introductions that people in your network suggest to you. You don't have to meet in person, but sometimes a quick interaction online can lead to interesting outcomes.

Everywhere you go and in everything you do, be on the lookout to grow your network with vibrant and interesting people. Make those short interactions into a lasting connection by using social media to stay in touch. Connect with people who are different from you to expose yourself to new ideas.

Actions and Ideas

To build your network consistently over time, ask yourself these questions:

Have you connected with everyone in your smartphone contacts list? Your colleagues? Your team members? The leaders at your company and in your industry?

Take a look at your calendar for the coming week or month. Who will you be meeting with? Connect with them in advance through the social media platform(s) of your choice.

Do you have a framework for accepting or declining invitations you receive in each social network? Thinking through who's a yes and who's a no in advance will save you time and build your network more strategically.

Do you introduce your connections in the right way, e.g., asking people separately in advance if it's okay to make the introduction? Be kind to your network and ask for their permission first.

Are you making a conscious effort to increase the bridging capital in your network—people who are different from you who could bring new perspectives and ideas?

CHAPTER 7

Be Creative, Innovative, and Speculative with Your Content

Success in social media is all about sharing quality content. The centerpiece of your social media strategy is the content you create yourself or curate from others. No matter how much technology enters our lives, people gravitate towards content that helps them make their lives better and entertains them in the process. Whether you are curating the content of others in a specific focus area or creating your own original content, it's important to share the very best content that you can. Don't share content just for the sake of sharing something. Share only the best content you can find or create.

Start by deciding on a few content areas you want to focus on, ideally two or three. Is it industry trends? Is it technology? Is it leadership? Whatever areas you choose should support your overall goals for your social media activity. If you're looking to leap to a higher-level job, for example, you'll want to highlight your leadership capabilities by sharing lessons you've learned, how you think about leading teams, and the results you've achieved.

My area of focus, not surprising in light the topic of this book, is social media for growing careers and companies. In addition, I share content related to leadership. And when I worked in the corporate world, I focused on sharing company news, especially if it aligned with my other areas of social media and leadership. Now that I work for myself, my clients, and my readers, I also share about my community roles that relate to social media and leadership at one of my alma maters.

The three words to guide your content creation or curation are to be creative, innovative, and speculative. Before you post content, ask yourself if it meets one or more of those criteria. If it doesn't, keep editing, iterating and improving. Let's dive into the meaning of each one, along with some examples.

Be Creative

Being creative essentially means to try new approaches to your content to see what resonates the most with your communities. What content do people respond to the most? What gets the most likes? The most comments? The most shares? Ask yourself why that might be. Try posting variations on the theme of what people engage with. Try different types of posts to see how people respond. Try various types of pictures and videos.

Observe content from others to see what attracts your interest and attention. Give some thought to what, specifically, caught your eye, so you can apply it with a personal touch to your own work. Don't be afraid to borrow ideas from others and make them your own with your unique perspective. Give credit where credit is due, and add your point of view to create something new.

As the bestselling writer Jeff Goins says in his book, *Real Artists Don't Starve: Timeless Strategies for Thriving in the New Creative Age*, "stop trying to be original."[54] He says, "Creativity is about learning to rearrange what has already been said in a way that brings fresh insight to old material."

Your content may also be more creative if you try to achieve multiple objectives from each piece of content you create. It's not possible to do it with everything, but strive to achieve more than one objective with each post you make.

John Stancliffe, a digital marketing leader in the corporate world, puts it well as a content marketer who creates material that helps promote products and services. "My rule before developing any sort of asset is questioning whether or not it will meet one or more key values: entertain, inspire, and educate. Hitting all three is all the better, but if it doesn't hit on one, it's time to go back to the messaging strategy."

As part of attracting attention for your content, make sure every social media post has a visual. It can be a video, a photo, a group of photos, or an infographic. Tweets that have images get 150% more retweets than text-only tweets.[55] Facebook posts with images get more than two times the amount of engagement than text-only posts.[56]

The best photos and videos are often the ones you take yourself. They display your unique view of the world, giving your content a more authentic feel. You also have the rights to your images.

Sometimes you need more than your own creativity can supply in the way of visuals. You can find royalty-free images by searching online, although the quality might not be at the level that matches your professionalism. I recommend checking out the good quality images you can buy from outlets like Canva or iStock by Getty Images.

What about memes? Most often a humorous image or video that is shared rapidly through social media, memes can also be informative, inspirational, or enlightening. Although the funniest memes sometimes go viral, they may strike a chord that is not the most suitable for work. Humor can often be misinterpreted or reflect poorly on you. Content you post and share is searchable forever. Stick with memes on the informative and inspirational side of the spectrum. Anything uplifting about leadership is usually a safe bet.

In your content and your images, think about the diversity of your communities. Be sure your content and visuals are inclusive and representative of a wide range of people. I subscribe to the view of Shonda Rhimes in her television writing, where she says, "I am making TV look like the world looks."[57]

When I bring other people's ideas into my writing and quote their work, I strive to include both women and men, as well as a variety of people representing multicultural communities whenever possible. The more people who can "see" themselves in your work, the bigger an audience you will reach and the greater impact you will have. In addition, you'll be doing your part to create a more inclusive world full of opportunities and inspiration for everyone.

One of my blog posts was about six ways social media can help you prepare for an initial business meeting.[58] The accompanying photo, which was part of my iStock subscription, focused on an African-American man shaking the hand of a white women, with another person looking on. My intent was to choose a photo that represented a few different groups of people. In addition, I believe the inclusive photo was one of the reasons why an African-American employee resource group retweeted the post to its membership, sharing my ideas with a broader audience in the process.

Be Innovative

Being innovative is about trying new approaches and being an early adopter of new features of social platforms. For example, LinkedIn added real-time video capability to its news feed. Instagram launched Stories for 24-hour content that disappears and therefore can be more playful and experiment than its regular feed. Twitter expanded its character count from 140 to 280.

It's a good idea to keep an eye on what's next. Examples include augmented reality, which may give us entirely new ways of projecting ourselves into a variety of contexts and locations. And artificial intelligence may give us more ways to automate our social media activity as individuals.

Sometimes what's new and different can be a twist on an existing theme or a new way of applying a concept to a different environment. For example, in thinking about how to build stronger relationships on LinkedIn, I wrote a blog post about why you should thank people for connecting. Not many people do this, so it can make you stand out in a new connection's mind to send a short, personalized reply with your thanks.

The big caveat to this approach is to never, ever pitch anything or ask for anything in your thank-you note. Don't ask for a job. Don't ask for a meeting. Don't ask for a referral. Don't do any of that. It's an immediate turn off and doesn't lead to the desired outcome of building a good relationship.

The new and different nature of this approach struck a nerve, because the article got more than 64,000 views. And although the article was posted more than a year and a half ago, I'm still getting comments and questions on it today.

What's a new and different take on what you're doing in your professional life that you could share in social media? Sometimes the simplest of career tips or productivity hacks might be of great interest and value to your network.

Be Speculative

Being speculative is about conducting experiments to see what works and what your audience engages with. In this way, you can create content that is completely unique to you and likely to be engaging for your audience.

For example, I've mentioned before that I wanted to test the data point that Carly Okyle cited in an Entrepreneur article about LinkedIn profiles that it takes about "20 LinkedIn posts every month to reach 60 percent of your audience."[59] So I did an experiment. I posted content every weekday for a month to see what I would learn.[60] Because LinkedIn is a social media platform for professionals, most content views are during the week.

As part of the experiment, I created a weekly content calendar. Mondays I posted from the employee advocacy program at the company where I worked. An employee advocacy program, which I'll cover in Chapter 9, is company-provided content that employees can tailor and share with their own social networks. Tuesdays I shared content from one of my favorite business publications, like Harvard Business Review, The Economist, or Inc. Wednesdays I found inspiration from articles based on one of my blog posts. Thursdays I found and used another employer advocacy program post. Fridays I shared a post from a colleague, an alma mater, or a professional association.

With this content calendar framework in mind, it wasn't as difficult as I anticipated to post every weekday. During early morning hours before I started work, it took about 10 minutes for most posts, and 30 minutes for articles.

What did I learn? Engagement increased each week, as measured by total views. My profile views went up too. By the end of the fourth week, profile views were up by 45 percent over the prior week.

Content re-shared by others got more engagement. When my first-degree connections re-shared my content with their networks, engagement peaked as measured by views and likes.

Analytics came in handy, because I could see whether a post got more engagement from my first- or second-degree network. Views are measured differently for posts and articles on LinkedIn.[61] Articles got fewer views than posts, but generated more likes. A view of a post means that, "someone saw your post in their LinkedIn home-page feed." The bar is higher for a view of an article, because it means that, "someone has clicked into and opened your article in their browser or on the LinkedIn mobile app."

Understanding this, it made sense that while views to my articles were lower than for posts, articles generated more likes. People had actually opened the link for articles.

Hashtags are important to make content discoverable. In my zeal to post frequently, I often forgot to include hashtags. That limited broader discovery of my content.

Posts on Tuesdays and Wednesdays got the most engagement. This is consistent with data showing it's best to post in the middle of the week on LinkedIn.[62]

The exception to this was if a post reached my second-degree network, then the day of the week didn't matter. And that's the most important thing I learned—the power of content that is re-shared beyond your first-degree connections.

If content is engaging enough for connections to share it with their networks, it reaches a much broader audience. It exposes your ideas to more people. And it creates opportunities to connect with more people who share common interests.

Most engagement was for posts about how to be a better leader and professional. This is consistent with LinkedIn being a social media platform for professionals in business. These posts were more likely to be positive and upbeat in nature, such as "How to be a Super Mentor."

And that's consistent with a study by two professors at the Wharton School, Jonah Berger and Katherine L. Milkman.[63] They looked at the most-shared articles for The New York Times. The content they found was shared the most was positive stories. As the professors said, "Content is more likely to become viral the more positive it is."

The three most positive words in the English language are happy, love, and awesome. This is according to Seth

Stephens-Davidowitz in his book *Everybody Lies: Big Data, New Data and What the Internet Can Tell Us About Who We Really Are*.[64] As a result, I use those words frequently in my social media content, both my own posts and my comments on others' content. Previously I had limited the use of those words, because they didn't seem to have enough gravitas in the corporate world. However, I believe sprinkling them throughout my messaging enables me to bring warmth to my communication and build stronger relationships.

The article about my experiment became one of my most viewed on LinkedIn to date, with almost 1,300 views. It was also one of my articles that got the most likes, comments, and shares. As an extension of this experience, I created my own spreadsheet to track the engagement with my content. This is another experiment that has yielded interesting and unique content for my network.

What is an experiment that you could conduct to learn more about a topic of interest to you and your network?

The Serendipity of Social Media

There's a serendipitous element of luck in social media. You never know exactly what will happen when you post something. It can also be a little like improvisation, or responding to something in the moment with absolutely no preparation. That's why it's important to keep tabs on what's happening with your content and be ready to jump into the conversation in new and different ways.

During my experiment about posting content every weekday, I tweeted an article about knowing when someone has true leadership skills. In the tweet, I asked about what leaders have been inspirational and why.

One colleague, Cynthia, responded by singing the praises of one of our other colleagues, Thomas. Cynthia did it in wonderful detail, mentioning specific leadership traits in an enthusiastic and engaging way.

Soon, Thomas joined the dialogue, with thanks and good humor. It was a great way to connect with people in my network.

What was even better was that I had an upcoming meeting with Thomas. I knew the conversation might be difficult due to the challenging subject matter. And in a moment of perfect serendipity, our Twitter conversation added a more upbeat and positive tone to our working relationship.

It goes to show that you never know how others in your network will respond to your content and what good outcomes may result. It also underscores a great mantra from social media author and podcaster Josh Ochs. He advises professionals and students alike to keep it "light, bright and polite" on social media, meaning upbeat, intelligent and respectful.[65]

As we all know, you can say the glass is half full or the glass is half empty. The state of the glass hasn't changed, but your perception and articulation of it creates emotional reactions in
your audience. Do you want them to be positive or negative? The more positive emotions you generate about your content, the better people will feel about *you*.

As you share content in social media, ask yourself if your material is creative, innovative, or speculative. Make sure to hit at least one of the three in every post by continuing to edit and iterate. If you can hit two or more, your content will be all the more engaging to your network. In this way you are building your personal brand and your reputation for thought leadership one post after another.

Once you know what content you're going to share, how do you do that in the best way possible? It's wise to be consistent, persistent, and efficient. That's what the next chapter will cover.

◆ ◆ ◆

Actions and Ideas

To create compelling content that builds your personal brand, be creative, innovative and speculative by considering the following:

Start by deciding on a few content areas you want to focus on, and ideally two or three. Is it industry trends? Is it technology? Is it leadership? Whatever content areas you choose should support your overall goals for your social media activity.

How creative can you be with your content? Can you meet two or more objectives each time you share in social media? What content seems to be resonating the most with your networks?

Do you approach your social media activity with an innovative mindset? Do you try new features when they are introduced by a social network? Are you creating short videos?

Are you trying new approaches with content in a speculative way? Is there an experiment you could conduct and write about?

Have you had any moments of serendipity in social media, where good things happened without your specifically trying? What did you learn? Is there a way to create more serendipitous moments?

CHAPTER 8

Be Consistent, Persistent, and Efficient in Your Approach

Once you know what content you want to share in a creative, innovative, and speculative way, how do you actually get it done? Here are three guidelines in your approach: be consistent, be persistent, and be efficient.

Being successful in social media is a long-term commitment that develops over time. You don't want or need something to "go viral" in order to boost your career. Your career won't be a one-hit wonder, and neither should your approach in social media. You want to share consistently so your network knows when they'll hear from you, post persistently so your efforts have a chance to build traction over time, and proceed efficiently so the majority of your time can be spent on building your career itself.

It can be easy to get discouraged when you post an article and very few people like it or comment on it. It can be hard to find reasons to keep going, to keep posting, and to keep experimenting. This chapter will help you see that you're in this for the length of your career journey, and how you will be rewarded by persevering.

Be Consistent

Being consistent means having a plan and a calendar, and executing against it. How often will you post, where will you post, and what will you post?

There are always new studies coming out on the ideal posting cadence for each social network. It's a good idea to keep tabs on the latest trends. Based in part on what the research says and what my own experience has revealed, here's the ideal cadence I developed during my years in the corporate world.

Each month I write at least two blog posts. During my corporate years, I wrote on weekend mornings, while my teens were sleeping in. It was a quiet time and our calendar was free of commitments. At times it felt overwhelming to come up with ideas for what to write about, to research the topic, to write the post, to find one or more good images to go with it, to edit it, to add hyperlinks, to proofread it, to post it, and to promote it. I was often unrealistic about the amount of time required, so I scaled back my original goal of a weekly post to a bi-weekly post.

Because LinkedIn is the center of my social media efforts, I strive to post an article every Wednesday, which is repurposed and refreshed from my personal blog. Most research says that posting in LinkedIn on Tuesdays, Wednesdays, and Thursdays is ideal, because that's when the most people are on the platform during the middle of the work week. The data I've collected, tracked, and analyzed for my own content tells me that these days are good, but what matters the most is the quality of the content. If the quality is good and valuable to people in your network and on LinkedIn, then the day of the week doesn't matter that much. Still, to maximize your efforts, target Tuesdays through Thursdays.

In addition to LinkedIn articles, I'll post a LinkedIn update one or two times a week. Content for posts includes my upcoming speaking engagements, my articles and blog posts, curated articles on social media and leadership, and shares of posts by others. On holidays, I share leadership quotes and a beautiful photo. In looking at my analytics, I discovered that holiday leadership quotes were among my most viewed content. I look for quotes that are timeless and inspiring. In the people I quote, I strive for a diverse group of people overall that represent both women and men, along with various multicultural groups.

On Twitter, I strive to tweet once or twice a day. The content mirrors LinkedIn posts, with a focus on brevity given the character limits on Twitter. If I'm attending an event or conference, I will live tweet the best soundbites from speakers. I'll keep an eye on the hashtag for the event and retweet a few that align most closely with my take on the event and the speakers. Each day I'll spend a few minutes to scroll through the home feed. I'll like tweets and potentially retweet one or two that align with my areas of focus on social media and leadership.

On Instagram, I try to do two or three posts each week and potentially one Story. Some research suggests up to one to two posts a day. Since the visual bar for quality is so high on Instagram, I post less often so I can focus on quality. Photos that are blurry or boring detract from anyone's image, so I try to avoid those. As I've covered in other parts of this book, Instagram is on the rise for visual branding. It's a great place to experiment with sharing highlights of your day in images, videos, and stories.

On Facebook, I try to do a weekly post, mainly to keep in touch with friends and family. Instagram has a feature where you can also post simultaneously to Facebook and to Twitter. For about a third of my Instagram posts I'll also share on Facebook. The reason I don't share all Instagram posts on Facebook is to keep some separation between the two. If I'm posting the same content on both networks, why would someone need to follow me on both? Photos that aren't as visually compelling as Instagram requires often work just fine on Facebook.

In Snapchat, I may play around in it on the weekends. Here, I learn from my kids about how to use it, what to do, and what not to do. There's no consistency here, nor does there need to be in this sandbox for learning and fun.

While I don't post on YouTube other than some of my speaking engagements that are available there, my former colleague Angelica Kelly has an interesting perspective. When she created her videos for her channel called You Brew Kombucha, people advised her to share the videos on a schedule over time. She did some research and reflection and ultimately decided to make them available all at one time.[66] It reminds me of how Netflix makes a whole season of a series available at once, so people can binge watch the episodes. It works for Netflix and it worked for Angelica.

Your social media cadence will be different, depending on what you want to accomplish, where you decide to play, and how much time you devote to it. You can experiment with different days of the weeks and different frequencies, both to see what works best with your schedule and what resonates the most with your networks.

If something doesn't feel right to you, don't force it. You want to come across as authentic, competent, and interesting. The best way to do that is to be true to what works for you. By establishing a consistent schedule and cadence to your posts, your networks will know when they'll hear from you, and they'll start to anticipate seeing your content.

Be Persistent

Being persistent means playing a long game. It means not getting discouraged when people don't seem to be resonating with your content. It means continuing to post on a consistent schedule and letting people know the content is there.

During the first two years of my blog, I didn't generate a great deal of traffic, which is typical for any new blog. While I loved the writing and content creating, I didn't like marketing my content. It felt too self-promotional and potentially annoying to people in my networks. I know how I feel when I get too many emails from a person or a company that are heavy handed in their sales tactics. I tune out. I unsubscribe. I delete. So for my blog posts, I generally did one tweet per post and that was it. As it turns out, this is a bad plan.

Oftentimes, people are afraid of using social media to boost their careers out of fear of doing something wrong or making a misstep or an embarrassing gaffe. However, the bigger threat is obscurity. No one will listen or pay attention to you unless you promote your content and your work. But how do you do that in an engaging and effective way?

One way to start is by using the analytics for each social platform. You can see what posts are the most successful, hypothesize about why, and conduct experiments to see what else you can learn.

My experiment to post every weekday to LinkedIn led me to repurpose my blog posts as LinkedIn articles, to help meet my daily posting goal. That exposed my blog posts to a larger audience—my connections on LinkedIn. There's also a great feature on the platform where you can share your article on Twitter and Facebook. I tweeted each article for broader exposure.

In addition, mentioning people in articles and posts helps to increase engagement. For LinkedIn articles, as an example, my goal is to link to at least three people and their work. I mention them in the LinkedIn post about the article. I include them in tweets with the article link. And I send LinkedIn messages to them to highlight key points that might be of interest to them. Oftentimes, they'll share the article with their networks, expanding the reach.

As you establish consistency in your social media posts, don't give up too soon. The first LinkedIn article I posted got 102 views, eighteen likes, one comment, and one share. My second article performed even worse with 84 views, four likes, and one comment. But I didn't give up. I kept posting an article, week after week, as I worked through my backlog of blog posts.

A few months later, my article on why you should thank people for connecting on LinkedIn struck a nerve.[67] A year and a half later it has gotten more than 64,000 views, 250 likes, and 34 comments. My corporate farewell article—a love letter to the amazing people I've worked with— attracted nearly 1,100 views, 183 likes, and 86 comments.[68] In analyzing all of my articles to date, the ones that seemed to relate the most to people were about topics that only I could write about. In some cases it was data I collected on my own and analyzed for trends I could share that would help my network. In other cases it was highly personal news, such as my departure from the corporate world and the launch of my social media consulting business.

Analyzing your analytics can help you do more of what jibes with your networks. Give yourself some runway by continuing to share in social media, even if you feel like you're not building up any traction. According to Jane Freeman in her book *The Business of Being a Writer*, only 10% of people reading your work will engage with it through likes, comments, or shares.[69]

My experience bears this out. Oftentimes, I'd be standing at the elevator at work and a colleague passing by would mention something they enjoyed in a recent article I posted. Or someone would invite me to speak to their mentoring circle or an employee resource group, because they'd read my articles. In all these cases, if someone hadn't said something to me in person, I wouldn't have otherwise known they were reading my content.

Give yourself a good six months to a year of consistently and persistently posting content. More than likely, you'll be happily surprised that you've begun to build a strong reputation based on the content you share.

Be Efficient

Being efficient means to fit your social media activity easily into your life. You're a busy person, between your professional and personal commitments. Think about the things you do on a regular basis that could make your content creation and posting a natural part of your day.

In my case, I read a lot. I read the news in the morning and throughout the day. I read while I'm walking on the treadmill. I read in the evenings before bed. And I especially love to read on weekends. As I do, I share relevant content in LinkedIn and Twitter, along with my perspective and the biggest takeaway I found. I try to mention the author of the piece, using their social media handle so they're notified of my comments. I'll include relevant hashtags so the content is more discoverable.

There are also nooks and crannies in the day when it's easy to share content. It could be during a short break, while waiting in line in the company cafeteria, or during halftime at a child's soccer game.

Media entrepreneur Gary Vaynerchuk has a brilliant strategy that's both efficient and compelling. He says to simply document your life, rather than trying to create perfect content.[70] He says, "When I say to put out six to seven meaningful pieces of content a day, pick up your smartphone, open Facebook Live, and just start talking about the things most important to you."

That takes very little time and effort above and beyond what you're already doing in the course of your day. To put that into practice, what could you share about your professional life today? Did you launch a new product, complete a critical project, or attend a conference? What did you do, accomplish or observe? Share that.

Just be sure what you're sharing is non-confidential and non-sensitive information that's okay to be shared in public. It's vitally important to know, understand, and follow your company's social media policies.

It can also make sense to break more time-intensive content creation into chunks of tasks you do over time. For my blog posts, I'd often try to do everything in one sitting, given my day job as a corporate vice president and a busy parent of two teens. That included coming up with ideas of what to write about, researching the topic, writing the post, finding good images to go with it, editing the post, adding and testing hyperlinks, identifying what words to tag, proofreading it, posting it, and promoting it. No wonder the process sometimes felt overwhelming. I began keeping an ongoing file of ideas as they occurred to me, so when I was ready to write I could easily choose from a number of existing ideas.

The bestselling writer Jeff Goins spoke about time management in a podcast conversation with Chandler Bolt who hosts the Self Publishing School podcast.[71] Jeff says he maintains three buckets: ideas, drafts, and edits. As each bucket fills up, it's easier to move among the three at different time periods, rather than trying to knock out each bucket in a single sitting.

It reminds me of a wise writing teacher, Marnell Jameson at UCLA Extension, who recommended that we put our work aside for a day—or at the bare minimum for an hour—before picking it up again to edit it with fresher eyes. With longer-form content like blog posts and articles, breaking work into chunks may not feel like the fastest move, but it *is* efficient.

You can also chunk up blog post writing and do two or more posts in a single sitting. This works the best for me when I'm writing on a topic that is too long for a single post and I need to break it into multiple parts, as I did for my social media research.[72] This strategy can work for all of your content, such as writing out your tweets for the week all in one sitting.

For the greatest efficiency, you'll want to make a social media editorial calendar. To keep it simple, you can create a document in Microsoft Excel or in an app such as Evernote. Make a chronological list of things you're doing each month of the year. Combine those with external calendar dates such as holidays and major announcements your company may be making, like quarterly earnings or product launches.

Hashtag holidays can also be a fun addition. Before there were hashtags that helped make content findable and discoverable in social media, organizations created holidays, such as World Health Day, to engage people around causes. Hashtag holidays grew in part out of these special dates

Sprout Social has a good calendar of hashtag holidays on its website[73] and there are others available through a search. For example, January 28 is #FunAtWorkDay, March 8 is #InternationalWomensDay, June 30 is #SocialMediaDay, August 9 is #NationalBookLoversDay, September 30 is #InternationalPodcastDay, and October 16 is #NationalBossDay.

Some of these hashtags might lend themselves to sharing content relevant to your areas of focus. You could weave in elements of your workplace culture, your favorite business book or podcast, and your best bosses.

Another efficiency trick is to keep a list of relevant hashtags you use often as a note in your smartphone. I maintain mine in a hashtag note in my Evernote app, which keeps all of my notes organized in a digitally accessible way. This is especially helpful for Instagram, which allows up to thirty hashtags per regular post and up to ten in a Story. You can simply cut and paste the hashtags you want to use into your post, without having to retype them all.

Speaking of hashtags, you can also create your own

hashtag or hashtags that you use consistently with your content. One great example is John Stancliffe, a digital marketing leader in the corporate world. He often uses the upbeat #KeepUpTheAwesome in content he posts on LinkedIn, Twitter and Instagram.

Yet another efficiency hack might seem to go without saying, but be sure you have your relevant social media apps on your smartphone and any other devices you use. I keep mine in a "social media" folder on my iPhone so it's easy to tap into them wherever and whenever I have a few free minutes.

You can keep experimenting with ways to increase your efficiency and refine your approach over time. Let's turn to how social media can help you make the most of a business meeting, a networking event or a conference, or an important email you're sending. Chapter 10 will also provide more ideas about how you can more easily fit social media into your life.

Prepare for an Initial Business Meeting

Do you have a method for how you prepare for an up-coming business meeting with someone you'll be meeting for the first time? You'll probably set objectives, create an agenda, and think about the information you want to share.

You can also take it one step further in social media to set your meeting up for success. Social media gives you valuable opportunities to learn more in advance about the person, or people, you'll be meeting. It opens a new window on what's important to someone and how he or she thinks. With social media, you can take a few minutes to get to know someone's career, their professional interests, and what they have in common with you.

Start with a Google search. You can search on the person's name, as well as the person's name along with their current employer or other keywords related to your meeting topic. Look at the first few screens to get a sense of the person, and visit a few of the links. Are they well-known in their field? Have they been quoted in the media recently? Been in a YouTube video?

Next visit their LinkedIn profile. Focus on their current role and the problems that person is solving in their work. Consider how that connects with your meeting objectives. See what other jobs they've held, what groups they're part of, and where they went to school. Read any recommendations people have written to get a better sense of who they are. See if you have any connections in common. If it's a really important meeting with a lot at stake, you could get insight in advance from a mutual connection.

After LinkedIn, look at their other social media activity. Are they active on Twitter, Instagram, or Facebook? Briefly visit those sites to round out your view of what's important to this person.

Read their blog, if they have one. Check out the most recent three posts, to see what they're currently focused on. Scan previous posts for topics that might be relevant to your upcoming meeting. If they don't have their own blog, see if they've posted articles in LinkedIn that would give you similar insight.

Once you have a sense of what you might have in common, or what's especially interesting to you about this person, send a personalized LinkedIn connection request. You can mention your meeting and that you'd like to connect in advance. This helps better establish the relationship, and it may prompt the person to view your profile and learn more about you. Make sure you've put your best foot forward in your profile. Any recent content you've posted should advance—or at a minimum not detract from—your meeting agenda and objectives.

Comment on their content. In your research, see what posts stand out to you as especially salient to your upcoming meeting. You can like and comment on a recent piece of content that is aligned with your meeting topic. And if it would be valuable to your own network, consider sharing it more broadly.

These actions will enable you to know your audience much better and help foster a positive working relationship from the very beginning. Just remember to keep it lighthearted in both your virtual and real-life interactions. Don't like or comment on *too* much material, and don't bring up subjects that your new business acquaintance might consider too personal or intrusive.

Make the Most of a Networking Event or a Conference

When you attend a networking event or a conference to add to your professional network and knowledge, do you set a social media goal? By being active on social media before, during, and after a conference, you can amplify the learning, expand your network, and further your reputation as a thought leader.

I've been fortunate to attend a number of amazing conferences, from professional associations such as the International Association of Business Communicators to thought leadership conferences such as TEDWomen and TEDx.

The first step is promotion. See if there's a social media plan posted on the conference website. When I attended the MAKERS conference for women's leadership, this came in a series of pre-event emails to attendees with sample messages and great images to share. Use the conference hashtags. That makes your content more discoverable to people who attend, and those who are following the conference on social media. Share pre-conference information in your social networks, perhaps about what you're most excited to learn or experience.

The second step is to connect. This is about getting to know new people you can learn from and exchange ideas with. Check out the attendance list in advance. If anyone already in your network is attending, you can reconnect as well as identify new people you want to meet. Be active in the event app—or in a social media group. Add your picture and key info to your app profile. Send messages to people you want to meet in person. Aim to introduce yourself to five to ten new people at each session. A goal to say hello to a focused number of people makes connections meaningful and manageable. To make the relationships last, you can send personalized LinkedIn invitations and/or follow people on Twitter or Instagram.

The third step is to share. This is all about sharing valuable content with your social networks, in alignment with your areas of focus. Post key learnings and sound bites in real time. Try tweets with key talk points. Share links to any conference recaps that are provided.

Consider writing a blog post about the experience. Speakers at TEDWomen were so moving that I blogged about my experience and what I took away from it.[74] After I attended the SHAPE conference, a technology and entertainment expo, I wrote a blog post about how to live tweet an event.[75] I realized that what seemed intuitive to me was actually a specific set of actions that might be helpful to others who want to live tweet an event but aren't sure exactly what to do or how to get started.

There are several other actions you can take after a conference to share what you learned, increase the impact, and grow the new network connections you made. To start, you can share a summary post with your colleagues and appropriate groups in your company's social intranet. You can connect with people you met on social media if you didn't do it during the conference. Lastly, you can commit to taking one new action based on what you learned. Share your new knowledge in social media, and do some follow-up posts over time that show how the new information is making a difference in how you do your work every day. The gem you picked up at a conference may be able to help others in your network.

Make an Email More Effective by Checking Social Media First

Before you send an important email, take one additional step after you edit for brevity, spell check, and proofread your work. This simple strategy can increase the impact of your message—whether you're asking someone for a favor, inviting them to speak at an event, requesting a reference, or making any number of asks. This simple strategy could tilt the scales toward a positive response. What is it? It's checking your recipient's latest social media activity.

There are three reasons for doing this. The first reason is that you may see recent updates that change your approach. Maybe your recipient has started a new job, been promoted, received an award, or spoken at a conference.

Those are great accomplishments to congratulate the person on, in a genuine and authentic way.

Here's a story that illustrates this. I advise never to send someone spam, otherwise known as an unsolicited pitch for business or a job. It's especially important not to do this right after you connect with someone on LinkedIn. These messages generally aren't worth the time to read and respond to, especially the jargon-filled ones where it's difficult to know what the person or business actually does.

But someone recently followed up his pitch for a meeting with a note that said, "I just noticed it looks like you left your company recently. I apologize for not checking that first. Congrats on your new venture! That sounds exciting."

He had actually looked at my LinkedIn profile, I assume, and saw that I recently launched my business called The Carrelle Company to help people grow their careers and companies through digital branding in social media. His message was kind enough and human enough that I decided to respond. His is one of the few pitch messages I've ever answered. The door is cracked open in a friendly way. That wouldn't have happened if the sender hadn't looked at my social media. And who knows what might transpire in the future. We're all connected and on paths that could converge in the future, in ways we can't even imagine today.

The second reason to check in on someone's social media pages before contacting them is that you may learn something that helps strengthen your relationship. When someone you've worked with previously reaches out to you to ask what's new, find out what they've been up to before you respond.

A few years ago I got a note like that from Karie Willyerd, who is the Chief Learning Officer at Visa. She is a fabulous speaker I invited to a few DIRECTV leadership events when I led corporate communications. Was I ever glad I checked her social media before responding. At the time she had just released a new book called *Stretch*, about lifelong learning and future-proofing your career.[76] That gave me the opportunity to congratulate her in my reply and learn more about her ideas.

In addition, you may gain insight into what's important to your recipient, and you may be able to appropriately connect your interests with theirs. Maybe you share a passion for a charitable cause, have a colleague in common, or are reading similar books.

But don't go overboard. Someone sent me a message recently that was over the top with praise for my blog, including examples from multiple posts. It was a bit jarring a few paragraphs later when the pitch for new business emerged. It had an inauthentic tone, and it did not motivate me to respond.

The third reason to keep an eye on others' social media sites is that you may find out there's a better time to send your message. Are you seeing beautiful vacation photos on Instagram? If they aren't hashtagged as #latergrams —meaning they weren't taken in the present moment— then you might want to hold off on your message until the person returns home. They could be more receptive then.

Maybe they're in the middle of a big work event and they're sharing it in social media. That could mean they don't have time to give your message the attention you'd like. When you do send your message, you could mention the event and your impressions of it, along with your congratulations.

Or maybe they're dealing with a challenging personal issue like a family member in the hospital. That's another reason to hold off on your message. If your message is urgent, at the very least you can acknowledge the situation and offer your support.

One caution is to take a lighthearted approach in your message so it doesn't appear that you're cyberstalking the person or that you inadvertently make them feel like you're invading their privacy. Be friendly, sincere, and brief.

There's mostly an upside to knowing your audience, what they've been doing lately, and what's important to them, which is what their recent social media activity can tell you.

As you become consistent, persistent, and efficient in your social media approach, you'll come to see that social media can become a natural and simple part of everything you do in your career and your life. Rather than viewing it as something separate and distinct, use social media as one more tool in your career toolkit to amplify the good work you're doing every day.

As you promote your career in social media, you will be more successful by bringing others along for the ride, which is the subject of the next chapter. When you build up your career, your colleagues, and your company on social media you will reap even more benefits through the principles of reciprocity and generosity.

Actions and Ideas

In creating a consistent, persistent, and efficient approach to your social media, ask yourself the following:

Are you consistent in how often and what types of content you share? Do you have a plan and a calendar, and do you execute against it? How often will you post, where will you post, and what will you post?

Are you tenacious in committing to your posting schedule, whether or not you're seeing significant engagement from your network? Are you willing to give yourself a runway to build up engagement with your network over time?

Are you efficient in how you conduct your social media activity? Do you batch similar tasks? Create blog posts in sets? Use hashtags consistently so your content is more discoverable and connected to you? Have you thought about creating your own unique hashtag?

Do you use social media to prepare for a business meeting or a networking event? Do you look at the social profiles of people you'll be meeting for the first time to get to know them?

Before you send an important email, do you check the person's social media activity first so you can tailor your message?

CHAPTER 9

Hit the Social Media Trifecta

Social media is all about reciprocity. This is one of the six principles of persuasion in the classic book by Robert Cialdini called *Influence: The Psychology of Persuasion*.[77] Essentially, the principle of reciprocity means that if someone gives something to us, we view it as a debt we are obligated to repay. Although Cialdini's book predated social media when it was first published in 1984, the principle of reciprocity underlies much of our behavior on social networks.

As humans, we want to return favors. If you highlight and share the accomplishments and ideas of your colleagues and the people in your social networks, they are likely to do the same for you.

Be sure to do it with a spirit of generosity. Don't keep score. As Wharton professor Adam Grant says in his book *Give and Take: A Revolutionary Approach to Success*, people who are givers do better than people who are takers in the game of life and business.[78]

Ruby Guzman, a managing partner at Organic Events in Southern California, is a great example of a giving spirit. "Successful people on social media are authentic and engaging," she says. "They actively engage with their followers by responding to questions and comments. They create and participate in conversation. They also post creative and relevant content that appeals to their followers." Ruby acts with this spirit in both her real life and social media interactions with people, increasing her impact in her work.

"Charity is the fastest way to get rich," the hip-hop sound engineer known as Young Guru said to me when I got the opportunity and the thrill of a lifetime to interview him on stage at a work event. In speaking about creativity and reinvention, he emphasized bringing the positive to everything you do—and doing great things for others with a giving spirit. His implication is that your generosity will come back to you in the form of various opportunities.

The spirit of giving is evident in how Tina Oppenheim Quinn, a life and leadership coach, describes people who engage with others unusually well. "Successful people on social media create helpful, informative, engaging, or inspiring content," she says. "They leave the conversation with the other person being more informed, inspired to change or take action, or feeling better."

Sharon Vogel, a communications strategist and consultant in Canada, emphasizes the importance of engaging with your network from their point of view. "Engage in a personal way that is meaningful to connections —whether it's sharing expertise on a hot topic, insight or lessons learned, or something funny or clever that will produce a good belly-laugh!" In our fast-paced work world, humor can be in short supply. If you take a lighthearted approach to your social media, put yourself in the shoes of your network, and make them laugh, people in your network will look forward to your posts.

To put a spirit of generosity into practice, go for a social media trifecta. Group your content strategy into thirds. The first bucket is your career, where you build your personal brand. The second is your colleagues, where you boost the people in your network. The third is your company, where you bolster your employer's brand.

Your Career

What Successful People Do in Social Media so far has focused on boosting your own career through social media. You've learned why it's important to do so consistently, how to get the personal and professional blend right in social media, how to define your personal brand, how to pick which social networks to invest your time in, and how to make your content compelling.

It's important to remember that everyone on this planet always asks themselves, what's in it for me? That's what's also known as the "WIIFM" question. So when you're sharing about your career or topics related to your industry or functional area, remember to ask yourself how that information will help your network. Think about how it will help your colleagues further their own careers. Consider how it will make their lives better or easier.

Just as no one enjoys being in a conversation where the other person talks about themselves the entire time, no one enjoys someone's social media feed that only tells you how great they are, post after post. Even "humble-brags," the seemingly modest statements that draw attention to a person's achievements, can get wearing after too many of them. If you post about receiving an award, for example, think of a way to share the credit, thank your team, or bring attention to a larger issue related to the award.

The humblebrag is also related to the concept of "flexing," or as the Urban Dictionary says, "to show off, to gloat, or to boast." It's a fine line between sharing what you're doing and being perceived as bragging, boasting, or flexing. Some experiences just don't belong on social media, like the time you may have been lucky enough to fly on a private jet. The question to ask yourself is how will people in your network feel about your post? Will they be excited for you? Or will they be envious and therefore turned off by your content? Ask yourself how you might feel viewing the content if someone else posted it, and you'll have your answer.

If you do find yourself bitten by the jealousy monster when viewing others' social media feeds, some of the best advice comes from Allyson Rener, president of Murphy O'Brien, a public relations and digital agency focusing on luxury lifestyle, travel and real estate. "Run your own race," she says. "You don't know the backstory when you're looking at people's social media feeds." You may only be seeing someone's highlights reel, and not the more difficult moments in their day.

Along those lines, it *is* possible to post *too* frequently. Sometimes seeing multiple posts from someone in the same day—when they're clearly not live tweeting an event or something similar—makes me wonder how they have time to get their main work done.

Make it clear from your social media activity that you are dedicated to your career, your colleagues, and your company. If you can get all three into a post, you've gone a long way toward developing positive feelings with your colleagues and potentially seeding some reciprocal behavior where others will sing your praises. And that's much more enjoyable and engaging than someone singing their own.

Your Colleagues

People love to be caught in the act of doing something good. Appreciation and praise happen far too infrequently in the work world. Social media gives you the perfect platform to highlight the good work of your colleagues. I use that term broadly, to include your company leaders, supervisors, peers, direct reports, and anyone else you work with on a regular basis.

Social media can be a good avenue to get to know your company's leaders, in a way you might not be able to do in the day-to-day operations of the business. If your workday doesn't often bring you into contact with company leaders, think about which ones you admire and which ones you'd like to get to know better. See what social media platforms they're on. Are they big into Twitter? Often on Instagram? More likely on LinkedIn? Take some time to observe the type of content they post. Then start to like and comment on it. In your comments, you can mention what stood out to you and relate it to your perspective. You could even share their content with your networks, if it relates to your focus areas. The caveat here again is not to do this *too* frequently. No more than once a week is a good idea and should be the maximum.

You can also strengthen your relationship with your supervisors by amplifying their content in social media. Be sure to do it in an authentic and genuine way, so it fits with the other content you share and wouldn't be perceived by others as overly obsequious, or simply seeking favor by questionable means.

Social media is a great place to strengthen peer relationships, which may be fraught with a competitive element as you all seek to grow your careers. By highlighting their good works and good deeds in an authentic way, you can foster stronger relationships over time.

When your team members notch a big win, social media is a great place to thank them publicly, in addition the recognition you may do in person. Be sure to include everyone who was part of the effort. Share your perspective on why their work was so important, the specific actions people took to make it happen, and the sacrifices they may have made along the way. This will build goodwill among your team. It will also help you be a talent magnet for other people who will want to be on your team in the future.

"Interacting with people's social media posts is a form of recognition," Charles Miller, a digital executive based in New York, told me. That's why he engages frequently with social media content from his colleagues and members of his network. He is also able to share business stories that are curated from the people he follows, often giving credit for the "finds."

You can apply these same principles to anyone else you work with—or anyone you want to get to know better. Notice what they're doing and share it with enthusiasm in your social networks.

Your Company

As an employee, you can be a proud brand ambassador for your company. Employee advocacy programs make it easy to do this. They also hit all three of your content buckets—you can promote yourself, your colleagues, and your company all at the same time.

In these programs, companies empower their employees to be brand ambassadors. You can share official news and information about the company and its brand through your personal social media channels. You'll generally find ready-made content to promote your company's brand and your colleagues. That also helps you be more efficient. If you maintain a personal blog and write a post that may be beneficial to your fellow employees, you can share it with your employee advocacy team to see if they'd be interested in including it as content.

Employee advocacy programs continue to grow and expand, with more companies offering them and with current programs adding new features. A group called JEM Consulting studies employee advocacy programs. Its latest study includes responses from more than 150 mostly U.S.-based companies. It pointed to the growth in employee advocacy adoption, which was up by more than 25% over the previous year. The most popular social networks are Facebook, Instagram and Twitter. YouTube grew dramatically by 35% in its use year over year —to 43% of respondents' employees using it.

According to Jen McClure, CEO of JEM Consulting, "We attribute this shift to the increased variety of industries and type of organizations adopting employee advocacy, as well as the expansion of business objectives for these programs."[79]

"We're seeing that all types of organizations are using visual media effectively," McClure also says, "especially online video, which was one of our key recommendations from last year's study." This fact underscores the popularity of video and the growth of video usage in social media that attracts the most engagement.

A related trend is the expansion of personal branding and thought leadership beyond a company's leaders. "The more people on your team who are building their brands and, by extension, your company's brand," says Forbes contributor John Hall in an article about PR trends," the more opportunities you have to distribute content and connect with your audience."[80]

One caveat with employee advocacy programs is to make sure the company content you share in your personal social media channels is relevant to your professional and personal networks.

Don't force something that isn't a fit. If it doesn't feel right, don't share it. A respondent to my social media survey said they didn't use their employee advocacy program because, "the content they produce is not 'share-worthy.' It's spun too much from a PR perspective."

You can look at how previous posts performed to assess how interested your networks may be in the content. I found that posts I made from an employee advocacy program performed well in LinkedIn and Twitter, but not so well in Facebook. That makes sense since my Facebook friends tend to be more personal in nature and probably less interested in the day-to-day news at my employer, unless it's something that directly affects them.

Here are the ways to make the most of your employee advocacy program. To start, download the app. Make it easy to share content by putting the app on your mobile devices. You can use snippets of time during the week to review and share content.

Choose content categories that support your professional goals. Align your own social media strategy with the available content categories. For example, you could focus on your company's business strategy, the customer experience, the employee experience, career strategies, or community engagement, to name a few.

Customize your feed for your content categories. Once you know what types of content you want to share, see if you can customize the content you see. This will make the process more efficient as you choose what to share.

Select the social media platforms you want to post on. Assess how the available content lines up with the platforms where you're most active for professional purposes.

Keep looking before you link, as I discussed in Chapter 3. Just as you shouldn't link to other social media content without reading it first, you should first read a company-provided message thoroughly. Make sure it reflects well on your professional brand before sharing it.

Tailor company-provided messages to your voice. You can use the company-provided messaging to share links, or you can edit it to sound closer to your own voice. Just be sure the edits you make reflect positively on your company.

Share your pride in your company or organization. Let your enthusiasm for your company shine through. Whether you love the employee experience, the products and services, or everything about your organization, share that sentiment.

As always, follow your company's social media guidelines. Make sure to follow the spirit and the letter of the guidelines. When in doubt, err on the conservative side. While you're acting as a brand ambassador of your company, that holds you to a higher standard.

Target a few posts each week. Sprinkle your company's posts among a broad variety of content you're sharing. Don't go overboard with excessive sharing. Since it's company-related content, post it on weekdays. Your platform may enable you to schedule sharing in advance to post at a specific time.

Share social content from colleagues. Keep an eye on content from colleagues who also engage in the advocacy program. Share their content if it fits with your overall goals.

Experiment and refine your approach. Check the analytics for each of your social platforms to see how your community is engaging with content from your company. Make adjustments based on that, and keep fine-tuning as you go.

What if your employer doesn't offer an employee advocacy program? Make a pitch to your corporate communications team. Here's a data point you could share. According to a Nielsen study, consumers see recommendations from friends as *the most* credible form of advertising—as much as 83%. And "employees are now your most credible spokespeople," communications expert Shel Holtz said when writing about the Edelman Trust Barometer.[81] The importance of employee voices continues to be strong.

By focusing in equal parts on your career, your colleagues, and your company in your social media content, you put the principle of reciprocity in play. You increase the likelihood that others will engage with and amplify your content by sharing it themselves. You ease up on the focus on yourself, which may be a relief for those who consider themselves more introverted or who simply feel uncomfortable with self-promotion. Also, for women and other groups who may be penalized for a perception that they're beating their own drums a little too loudly, this three-pronged strategy will help you stand out in a good way on social media.

Now let's pull together the last nine chapters with a look at how you can more easily fit social media into your life.

Actions and Ideas

To hit the social media trifecta of boosting your career, your colleagues, and your company, consider these questions:

Do you engage with and share the content of colleagues and your company with a spirit of generosity and as a good teammate?

Are you judicious in posting about your career, refraining from too much "humblebragging" and posting too frequently?

Do you find reasons to highlight the good work of your colleagues and your team members in social media?

Do you identify leaders at your company and in your industry that you want to develop relationships with? Do you have a plan for engaging with their social media content by liking and commenting on their content so you can build a relationship over time?

Are you a good brand ambassador for your company? Do you share company news that aligns with your subject areas of focus on social media?

Does your company have an employee advocacy program? Have you signed up for it and downloaded the app to your smartphone? Do you share content from it, tailored with your unique point of view?

CHAPTER 10

The Secret to Fitting Social Media into Your Life

We each have 24 hours in days that seem to get more full by the second. Careers, families, health, finances, friends, recreation and more compete for our time and attention. Our careers influence every other part of our lives, from a feeling of purpose and meaning to the financial rewards that enable us to provide for our families and the special times we spend with our loved ones.

You work hard in your career to make a contribution and achieve higher levels of responsibility and compensation. In addition to all of your efforts, making sure you're visible, connected, and on the radar of people who can make a difference in your career can accelerate your progression. Our professional reputation will increasingly influence how we get jobs, advance in our careers, and navigate transitions between jobs and careers.

The "value proposition," or the way to show value to your network, is clear for having a social media strategy. The bigger challenge is making the time for it. Like anything in life that is important but not urgent, social media can languish on the back burner of your busy life.

The solution is to make it a habit like any other, simplifying and automating where you can, and realizing you don't have to do everything in social media to make a name for yourself that opens more doors to opportunity. It's also a matter of starting, wherever you are, and building on your efforts over time.

Think of all the business protocols that have become a habit—ones you don't even think about as you go about your day. Take meetings as an example. If you're going to hold a meeting, what do you do? Best practices say you determine your objective for the meeting, identify the key decision makers who need to be there, develop an agenda, and get an invitation on people's calendars. You probably don't even think about those steps anymore, because they've become as innate as breathing.

The same can be said about social media. You can establish your own guidelines and protocols to make social media part of everything you do. Start by thinking about what you've done professionally over the last month. Have you spoken at an event? Attended a conference? Taken a course, whether it was online or in person? Traveled for a work meeting or an event? Joined a professional or trade group and attended a meeting? Completed a key project that can be shared in public? Participated in a company-sponsored charitable event? Seen an engaging video about your company or industry? Found a valuable article or podcast about your company or industry? Read a thought-provoking book about business or your industry? Come across an interesting post by a colleague or your company?

These activities and many more can be the foundation of social media content that documents the interesting and relevant things you are doing in your professional life. This is a strategy inspired by VaynerMedia CEO Gary Vaynerchuk that I covered in Chapter 8. His blog post called, "Document, don't create: creating content that builds your personal brand,"[82] had a big impact on me. "Documenting *is* creating content," he says. "It's simply sharing your career journey and what you're doing every day. And it's easy to do because you're just being yourself."

And being yourself is you at your most genuine and authentic. This is where your personality and your passions really shine through. And this is what is most engaging to others on social media—getting to know the real you in a professional sense.

In everything you do in your work life today, start by asking yourself if it can be shared publicly in social media. The big caveat to that is to make sure to never, ever share non-public and/or competitively sensitive information in social media. When in doubt, err on the side of caution and don't share. Even if you think something is okay to share in public, check that official company sources have shared the information publicly, or ask your supervisor for confirmation.

Career blogger Penelope Trunk said it well in her online course called Reach Your Goals by Blogging.[83] "Just don't write anything near where your 'security clearance' goes," she advised. While most people don't have security clearances, this is an apt analogy to keep confidential information confidential. Don't share it.

Once you've cleared that hurdle, then focus on what you're doing, what's interesting about it and why it could be valuable to your network. What specifically in the course of your day, your week and your month could you share that builds the career brand you want to be known for?

A quick photo or video clip along with a few sentences about what you did and why it's important and who you did it with, along with a relevant hashtag or two to make your content more discoverable, is all it takes. Then you simply rinse and repeat on a regular basis.

Some people I know do this really well. Jaime Lee is a real estate executive in Los Angeles who was the youngest president of the USC Alumni Association and the first Asian woman to hold the post. She was then the youngest person to be named a trustee of the university. She also serves on several civic boards and has two young children. Through it all, she shares what she's doing in regular posts to Instagram and Facebook. She posts interesting and fun photos that are engaging and illustrative of what she's doing during her busy days. She'll share leadership lessons she's learned in her career, along with events she attends and speaks at in the course of her work.

Patrick Auerbach is a master at Facebook and connecting with USC alumni around the world. As the university's associate senior vice president for alumni relations, Patrick is an amazing role model for engaging with alums. He chronicles his professional and personal lives with a very active Facebook presence. His success is evident in the amount of engagement he gets on his frequent posts and updates. He is even able to make the wait in the line outside The Original Pantry Café in Los Angeles, a quintessential L.A. experience, look like fun —from happy faces in line to the plaque describing the much-loved L.A. experience.

Both Jaime and Patrick have the ability to share content that makes you feel as if you were there and draws you into their lives. The sense of fun and adventure leaps off the screen. These are great examples of what Guy Kawasaki calls "the ability to make people feel like they are sharing the moment with you in social media."[84]

In recent months I've shared blog posts and LinkedIn articles, Facebook Live speaking engagements, the opening bell at the New York Stock Exchange as part of a professional association meeting I attended, interesting articles I read and podcasts I listened to, and my upcoming speaking engagements. Most of these posts only required taking a few photos or videos of the events and sharing key messages in my social networks. They tended to be squeezed into the nooks and crannies of busy days as well as evenings and sometimes weekends, forming the public side of work-related activities that can be shared in social media.

Maybe you read frequently, listen to podcasts, or watch TED talks. If they fit with the topics you usually share in social media, you can post those, along with your perspective on the work and a key takeaway. It's valuable to your network if you include a brief nugget of inspiration or information.

I've been known to tweet while walking on a treadmill or waiting in line. And at a conference or event, it's fun to live tweet a great quote from each of the speakers, along with a photo.

Having an editorial calendar is advisable, as I covered in Chapter 8. It doesn't have to be anything fancy or overly complicated. Take time as you're planning each month's and week's activities to identify what content you want to share in social media.

Beyond building your career through social media, there are other benefits to documenting your professional life socially. You're helping to build the brands of your company and your colleagues.

Employees are a trusted and credible source of information about their companies. Take that responsibility seriously and be sure you're communicating in alignment with your company's values, brand, and social media policy.

Along those lines, it's wise to use your own personal smartphone and laptop for your social media activity, rather than devices that belong to your employer. Be judicious about posts you make during official work hours, to avoid the perception that your social media activity is happening at the expense of delivering on your core job responsibilities. Of course, if you're posting to social media about a company event where it's okay to share it publicly, you can and should post in real time. To keep your work productivity and focus where it needs to be, only view your social media feeds at set times during the day when you're taking a short break.

Your social media activity can be a valuable input into your year-end performance assessment. It documents many of your accomplishments. You can add to quantifying their impact by the reach and the engagement of your posts.

As you think about the day and the week ahead, what are you doing, experiencing, and learning that you can share in social media?

There's no need to wait for the perfect moment. It will never come. And you might realize the perfect moment is actually right here, right now.

Being active in social media to grow your career is really about living your best life and sharing your insights and perspectives with others who can benefit from them. You can lift others up along the way and show what it means to be a leader of people and in ideas.

If you take one thing away, let it be this. Starting now, live the life you want to live—and share it on social media.

How to Handle Haters

It started innocently enough. Someone mentioned me in a tweet about a business-related dispute. So I read the tweeter's bio. I researched the issue. I realized there was nothing meaningful I could do in response.

Then the tweets came more frequently. Three, four and more times a day. It became harder to ignore the notifications on my Twitter app. I started to wonder if my non-response strategy was a good idea. In talking with some colleagues in the social space, we concluded that it was.

Still, it was painful being the subject of increasingly negative tweet after tweet, because usually I believe in responding.

This is especially true if it's a customer, and it's gratifying to help people solve issues. However, this particular case did not involve a customer.

The same as the schoolyard bully, the best response is often no response. If you act indifferently for long enough, the hater will eventually go away.

I was so excited when Janice Walters, the graphic designer who created the logo for my new business, The Carrelle Company, posted it to her Instagram. It's two letter C's, asymmetrically placed in a square, in white and grey lettering over a bright red background. Then I saw the first comment on the post— #subliminalboobs. Ugh. Oof. Who *was* this person? I immediately wanted to hit back and post an obnoxious comment of my own. What came to mind was #subliminalpervert. But I ultimately decided that no response was the best response. I wasn't going to let one silly person ruin my excitement about the new look and feel for my company.

But inappropriate and hate-filled comments concern me. They remind me of the actor Ashley Judd's TED-Women talk about online abuse spiraling out of control.[85] One of her tweets at a basketball game a few years ago incited a cyber mob of hate. Yet rather than responding to the haters themselves, she became an activist for a safe and free internet for everyone.

She had, from time to time, tried engaging people. She met with varying degrees of success. One person in particular had a refreshing response and actually apologized.

That made me think beyond the awful posts and comments themselves. What kind of pain must someone be in to post hateful and threatening material? What has happened to them to make them act that way? What are they most afraid of?

A Facebook friend posted recently that she was leaving the platform for a while. She was tired of the negativity around politics and felt the best solution was to step back.

The outpouring of encouraging comments was heartening, including the advice to ignore the haters and focus on the connections with friends and family. She still chose to take a break. But I'm glad she eventually came back.

Because we need positive voices. We need realistic optimism. We need civil dialogue. And we need empathy. Everyone is dealing with some kind of challenge, whether it's visible on the outside or not. So it's up to each of us to be kind, to be caring, and to be curious.

This is a strategy that has worked for Gary Vayner-chuck, CEO of VaynerMedia. Like Ashley Judd, he's engaged haters with respect for their views. He asks questions to better understand the underlying issue. He listens, and he creates a dialogue.

That's where your judgment comes in. Should you ignore or engage? Every situation is different, so what might work in one instance may not work in another. Try seeing things from another point of view. And see where that takes you.

This is also about exercising control where you can. You can't control the behavior of others, but you can control yourself.

Should You Respond or Not Respond?

Our incoming messages are exploding. There are LinkedIn messages. There are Facebook, Instagram, and Twitter notifications. Then there are emails, texts, and direct messages.

Just reading and responding to everything could be more than a full-time job. That applies especially to the ones asking for a 30-minute meeting to pitch a product or service.

That's why you need a strategy for when you do and don't respond. And I don't subscribe to the philosophy that no response is always the best way to say no. In our hyper-connected world, our humanity and good manners can too easily go by the wayside.

Sometimes it's because we can't help the person and we need to say no. In those cases, you could create a standard professional response you can copy, paste, edit and send to say you're not interested at this time. You don't have to respond again after that.

Some messages are easy not to respond to. They include the seemingly automated sales pitches that often come through LinkedIn. Then there are connection requests that are immediately followed by a sales pitch, again, often through LinkedIn and Twitter. There are connection requests in LinkedIn from people you don't know and that aren't personalized to explain why they'd like to connect with you. There are tweets that mention you as a way to draw you into an issue for which you can offer no meaningful response.

But some messages *do* deserve a response. And while it would be easy enough to ignore them, giving a response can set you apart and enhance your company's reputation.

A big example is customers of your employer who need help getting an issue resolved. You can and should respond to that customer right away. You can be the friendly, helpful, human face and voice they're looking for. You can help connect them with your company's customer care team for a rapid response. As always, do it in accordance with your company's policies on customer interaction and on social media.

An interesting data point is that 78% of people who complain to a brand in Twitter expect a response within an hour. In addition, 77% of people feel more positive about a brand when their tweet has received a response.[86]

Other messages that deserve a response are people from your alma maters, past and present employers, and other professional groups who ask for your advice or an introduction to a colleague for networking purposes.

Then there are connections, colleagues, and friends

who post valuable content. This is where you can read their link, like the content if it's something you want to be associated with, and leave a short and upbeat comment that adds a constructive observation to the dialogue.

Some messages fall in between. An example is a request to connect to one of your connections, without a clearly stated reason. A LinkedIn connection asked me to connect her to a colleague, to invite her to an event. I suspected it was a sales pitch and didn't want to spam my colleague. I asked the connection for more info. She never responded. That was the end of the conversation.

Suppose you do decide to respond to a message to decline a request and you get a response asking for something else. What do you do then? Simply realize that one response is sufficient and there's no need to continue the dialogue.

The one exception, though, is from a customer who needs your help. In that case, keep responding until the issue is resolved to the customer's satisfaction, because our customers are the lifeblood of our organizations.

Be a Social Superhero

Mentoring has always been important to me. When I was changing careers from a supply chain role into a corporate communications position, so many people took time for informational interviews with me. I'd ask about what they did every day, what they loved—and hated— about their careers, and what advice they'd give to someone looking to break in. At the time I didn't feel I had anything to offer in return.

That's why mentoring is so important to me. I'm happy to share my advice and perspective with people of all ages and career stages. In my corporate life, I led a number of mentoring circles, small groups of people who would address career topics in a supportive environment. In one of my mentoring circles, two of the participants, Norma and Shandria, invited me to come and speak to colleagues at their work site during a career development week.

If social media is all about reciprocity, as I've set forth in this book, then so is learning. During this site visit, I was filled with great ideas about leadership and service. Shandria even had my own bitmoji created as Social Media Woman. It's me in a Wonder Woman cape and gloves, with a Twitter choker and a LinkedIn belt.

I realized this had all come about because I started a side project I was really excited about spending my evenings and weekends doing—my blog exploring how people can use social media to grow their careers. One thing led to another and now I've launched my own business. I'm enjoying the process of growing it every day.

My Social Media Woman is now proudly displayed in a visible spot above my desk in my home office. It's an ever-present reminder that we all have super powers. We can all solve problems. We can all make our workplaces better every day.

If we set our mind to doing something, we can do it. *You* can do it. What will *you* do in social media to accelerate the course of your career?

Actions and Ideas

As you look to fit social media into your busy life as a habit like any other, think about the following:

Do you consider documenting your work day and what would be interesting and non-confidential to share with your networks?

How do you make social media part of the work events you attend?

What are some of the efficiencies you've found in your social media approach? How could you find more?

What is your plan to handle haters, or people who are less than positive in their social media interactions?

Do you have guidelines for what you do and don't respond to in social media?

What is the highest and best use of social media to build your career? What is the legacy you want to leave?

APPENDIX

10 Quick Start Steps for Your Social Media

If you want to get started right away on boosting your career in social media, here are 10 quick actions.

1. Follow your company's social media policy. Disclose your company affiliation. Don't share confidential information.

2. Decide what you want to be known for. Who do you want to be? What is your personal brand?

3. Pick where to play. Start with LinkedIn. Consider Instagram, Twitter, and possibly your own blog.

4. Build your network. Wherever you go and whatever you do, add people to your social networks.

5. Observe others' content to see what works. Scroll through your social feeds daily. See what content catches your eye.

6. Get to know leaders and colleagues. People you might not spend a lot of time with are often accessible in social media.

7. Mention and tag people. They will be notified of your posts and may be more likely to see and engage with your content.

8. Use hashtags. Make your content more discoverable with hashtags. You can even create your own unique hashtag.

9. Analyze your analytics. Check out the analytics on each platform to see what content gets the most engagement.

10. Experiment and learn. Try new things with your content. See how your network responds.

ABOUT THE AUTHOR

Caroline Leach helps people and organizations tell their stories. As a Fortune 100 Vice President of Corporate Communications and Marketing for more than a dozen years, Caroline founded The Carrelle Company to provide digital branding for people to grow their careers and companies through social media. The Carrelle Company was born on Labor Day 2018 from a blog Caroline launched on New Year's Day 2015. She writes, researches, consults, speaks, and teaches on this topic. When she's not discussing social media, Caroline enjoys spending time with her family at her home in the Los Angeles area. For more, visit carolineleach.com.

ACKNOWLEDGMENTS

So many people inspired my writing journey. My grandmother, affectionately called Graer Kate, encouraged me from the very beginning. My mom and dad, Chris and Harvey Place, filled their home with books for me and my sister, Katie Rogers. My uncle, Pete Martin, gave me a typewriter in kindergarten so I could write stories.

It has been a long and winding path to the creation of this book. Along the way I've been blessed to work alongside some of the most amazing and talented people in the corporate world and in my community. While there are too many to mention in this short space, I appreciate you and what I learned from you more than I can say. I am thankful for the social networks that enable us to keep in touch, across the distance of time and space.

Thank you to every person who read my blog and told me it helped them improve their career or their life. Thank you to every person who invited me to speak about what successful people do in social media. Thank you to everyone who encouraged me.

Thanks to Cat Spydell, my editor, for asking the right questions and helping make this book the best it could be.

Thanks to Janice Walters, my graphic designer, for creating a book cover that commands attention.

Thanks to Jessica Sterling, my photographer, for working her magic with lighting and camera angles.

2222

Thanks to my children, Cameron and Connor Leach, two wonderful people who slept in on weekend mornings as teens, giving me precious time to write.

Thanks to my husband, Kevin Leach, who always supports me in pursuing my dreams and encourages me every step of the way.

Everyone should be so lucky.

Caroline Leach
Los Angeles County
April 2019

YOUR SOCIAL MEDIA SUCCESS ROADMAP

with

50 Questions, Actions and Ideas
to Help Boost Your Career
through Social Media

A free workbook with space to write responses to the "Actions and Ideas" prompts at the end of each chapter is available as a free PDF download at **carolineleach.com**

NOTES

[1] Arnie Fertig, "How Headhunters Use LinkedIn to Find Talented Candidates: Tips to Make Yourself Findable," *Money*, May 5, 2017, https://money.usnews.com/money/blogs/outside-voices-careers/articles/2017-05-05/how-headhunters-use-linkedin-to-find-talented-candidates

[2] Number of Employers Using Social Media to Screen Candidates at All-Time High, Finds Latest CareerBuilder Study," CareerBuilder press release, June 15, 2017, http://press.careerbuilder.com/2017-06-15-Number-of-Employers-Using-Social-Media-to-Screen-Candidates-at-All-Time-High-Finds-Latest-CareerBuilder-Study

[3] Michael Fertik and David C. Thompson, *The Reputation Economy: How to Optimize Your Digital Footprint in a World Where Your Reputation is Your Most Valuable Asset* (New York: Crown Business, 2015.)

[4] Michael Sheetz, "Instagram inches ahead of Snapchat in popularity among teens: Piper Jaffray," October 22, 2018, https://www.cnbc.com/2018/10/22/instagram-ahead-of-snapchat-in-popularity-among-teens-piper-jaffray.html

[5] Joe Flint and Ben Fritz, "ABC Cancels 'Roseanne' Sitcom Hours After Star's Racist Tweet," May 29, 2018, https://www.wsj.com/articles/abc-cancels-roseanne-after-roseanne-barrs-tweet-about-valerie-jarrett-1527618053

[6] Football coach's tweet cost $1.6 million in lost donations," *KXLY.com*, November 17, 2018, https://www.kxly.com/news/football-coach-s-tweet-cost-16-million-in-lost-donations/871636525

[7] Caroline Leach, "Boost Your Career through Social Media, Part 1." Blog. *Ow to Build Your Career through Social Media,* April 10, 2018, https://www.carolineleach.com/boost-your-career-through-social-media-part-1/

[8] Dorie Clark, "What You Need to Stand Out in a Noisy World," *Harvard Business Review*, January 6, 2017, https://hbr.org/2017/01/what-you-need-to-stand-out-in-a-noisy-world

[9] Tim Ferriss, *Tribe of Mentors: Short Advice from the Best in the World* (New York: Houghton Mifflin Harcourt, 2017.)

[10] Tony Schwartz and Christine Porath, "Why You Hate Work," *The New York Times*, May 30, 2014, https://www.nytimes.com/2014/06/01/opinion/sunday/why-you-hate-work.html

[11] Definition of globalization in Investopedia, reviewed by Will Kenton, updated January 28, 2018, https://www.investopedia.com/terms/g/globalization.asp

[12] Otaviano Canuto, "How globalization is changing innovation," World Economic Forum, August 17, 2018, https://www.weforum.org/agenda/2018/08/globalisation-has-the-potential-to-nurture-innovation-heres-how/

[13] World Economic Outlook, 2018, International Monetary Fund, April 2018, https://www.imf.org/en/Publications/WEO/Issues/2018/03/20/world-economic-outlook-april-2018

[14] Elaine Pofeldt, "Are We Ready for a Workforce That is 50% Freelance?" *Forbes*, October 17, 2017, https://www.forbes.com/sites/elainepofeldt/2017/10/17/are-we-ready-for-a-workforce-that-is-50-freelance/#4367a2713f82

[15] Karie Willyerd and Barbara Mistick, *Stretch: How to Future-Proof Yourself for Tomorrow's Workplace* (New Jersey: John Wiley & Sons, Inc., 2016).

[16] Reid Hoffman, Ben Cashnova and Chris Yeh, "Tours of Duty: The New Employer-Employee Contract," *Harvard Business Review*, June 2013, https://hbr.org/2013/06/tours-of-duty-the-new-employer-employee-compact

[17] Philip Yuen, "The 7 Forces That Will Change the Way You Work," World Economic Forum, September 3, 2018, https://www.weforum.org/agenda/2018/09/here-are-seven-ways-your-job-will-change-in-the-future/

[18] Philip Yuen, "The 7 Forces That Will Change the Way You Work," World Economic Forum, September 3, 2018, https://www.weforum.org/agenda/2018/09/here-are-seven-ways-your-job-will-change-in-the-future/

[19] Guy Kawasaki and Peg Fitzgerald, *The Art of Social Media: Power Tips for Power Users* (New York: Penguin Group, 2014.)

[20] Carly Okyle, "18 Tips to Create Your Perfect LinkedIn Profile," *Entrepreneur*, April 4, 2016, https://www.entrepreneur.com/slideshow/307172

[21] Fast Company, September 2012, https://www.fastcompany.com/3010818/fast-company-from-cover-to-cover-jan-2012-to-dec-2012

[22] "Is There a Limit to the Human Lifespan?" *The Wall street Journal*, June 24, 2018, https://www.wsj.com/articles/is-there-a-limit-to-the-human-lifespan-1529892420

[23] Sarah Boseley, "Great Expectations: Today's Babies are Likely to Live to 100, Doctors Predict," *The Guardian*, October 1, 2009, https://www.theguardian.com/society/2009/oct/02/babies-likely-to-live-to-100

[24] Lynda Gratton and Andrew Scott, *The 100-Year Life: Living and Working in an Age of Longevity* (Bloomsbury: London, 2017.)

[25] "Future Skills: Get Fit for What's Next," Institute for the Future, 2018, http://www.iftf.org/fileadmin/user_upload/futureskills/downloads/IFTF_FutureSkills_Map.pdf

[26] Thomas Friedman, *Thank You For Being Late: An Optimist's Guide for Thriving in the Age of Accelerations* (New York: Farrar, Straus and Giroux, 2016.)

[27] Ariane Ollier-Malaterre and Nancy P. Rothbard, "How to Separate the Personal and Professional on Social Media," *Harvard Business Review*, May 26, 2015, https://hbr.org/2015/03/how-to-separate-the-personal-and-professional-on-social-media

[28] Caroline Leach, "How Professionals Can Build Their Careers through Social Media, Heather Rim Profile: Brand You." Blog. *Ow to Build Your Career through Social Media*, September 26, 2018, https://www.carolineleach.com/heather-rim-profile-brand-you/

[29] Caitlyn Dewey, "6 in 10 of You will Share this Link Without Reading It, a New, Depressing Study Says," *The Washington Post*, June 16, 2016, https://www.washingtonpost.com/news/the-intersect/wp/2016/06/16/six-in-10-of-you-will-share-this-link-without-reading-it-according-to-a-new-and-depressing-study/?utm_term=.e505680ce074

[30] David Gelles, "How to Be Mindful with Facebook," *The New York Times*, September 28, 2016, https://www.nytimes.com/2016/09/28/well/mind/how-to-be-mindful-with-facebook.html

[31] Michael Fertik and David C. Thompson, *The Reputation Economy: How to Optimize Your Digital Footprint in a World Where Your*

Reputation is Your Most Valuable Asset (New York: Crown Business, 2015.)

[32] Tom Peters, "The Brand Called You," *Fast Company,* August 31, 1997, https://www.fastcompany.com/28905/brand-called-you

[33] Clement Lim, "5 Steps to Building Your Personal Brand from Scratch," *Entrepreneur*, September 29, 2017, https://www.entrepreneur.com/article/298513

[34] Steve Chandler, *Reinventing Yourself: How to Become the Person You've Always Wanted to Be* (New Jersey: The Career Press, Inc., 2017.)

[35] Kevin Kruse, "Personal Branding Tips from Dorie Clark," *Forbes*, March 9, 2018, https://www.forbes.com/sites/kevinkruse/2017/03/09/personal-branding-tips-from-dorie-clark/#7f1e4a83591b

[36] Caroline Leach, "What's in a Name? The Carrelle Company is Born on Labor Day," Blog. *How to Build Your Career through Social Media,* September 5, 2018, https://www.carolineleach.com/whats-in-a-name-the-carrelle-company-is-born-on-labor-day/

[37] Dorie Clark, "How Women Can Develop—and Promote—Their Personal Brand," *Harvard Business Review*, March 2, 2018, https://hbr.org/2018/03/how-women-can-develop-and-promote-their-personal-brand

[38] 2018 BRANDfog Survey, *The Power of Social Media for Women Executives,* http://brandfog.com/survey/the_power_of_social_media_for_women_executives_2018.pdf

[39] Caroline Leach, "How to Be Your Best You Through Personal Branding." Blog. *How to Build Your Career through Social Media.* March 11, 2018, https://www.carolineleach.com/how-to-be-your-best-you-through-personal-branding/

[40] Carla Harris, *How to Own Your Power Presentation*, YouTube, March 5, 2014, https://www.youtube.com/watch?v=0rWmtyZXkFg

[41] Chandler Bolt, *The Getting Things Done Approach to Writing Your First Book with David Allen*, Self Publishing School Podcast episode 43, March 14, 2018, https://self-publishingschool.com/getting-things-done-david-allen/

[42] W³Techs World Wide Web Technology Surveys on Content Management Systems, December 1, 2018, https://w3techs.com/

[43] Carly Okyle, "18 Tips to Create Your Perfect LinkedIn Profile," *Entrepreneur*, April 4, 2016, https://www.entrepreneur.com/slideshow/307172#2

[44] LinkedIn website, About page, accessed January 17, 2019, https://about.linkedin.com/

[45] LinkedIn by the Numbers: Stats, Demographics & Fun Facts," Omnicore website, accessed January 17, 2019, https://www.omnicoreagency.com/linkedin-statistics/

[46] Twitter website, About page, accessed February 3, 2019, https://about.twitter.com/en_us.html

[47] "Twitter accounts with the most followers worldwide as of January 2019," *Statista; The Statistics Portal* website, accessed February 3, 2019, https://www.statista.com/statistics/273172/twitter-accounts-with-the-most-followers-worldwide/

[48] "Number of daily active Instagram Stories users from October 2016 to January 2019," *Statista: The Statistics Portal* website, accessed February 3, 2019, https://www.statista.com/statistics/730315/instagram-stories-dau/

[49] "Number of monthly active Facebook users worldwide as of 4th quarter 2018," *Statista: The Statistics Portal* website, accessed February 3, 2019, https://www.statista.com/statistics/264810/number-of-monthly-active-facebook-users-worldwide/

[50] "Video will account for an overwhelming majority of internet traffic by 2021," *Business Insider Intelligence*, June 12, 2017, https://www.businessinsider.com/heres-how-much-ip-traffic-will-be-video-by-2021-2017-6

[51] "You Brew Kombucha," *YouTube channel*, accessed February 2, 2019, https://www.youtube.com/channel/UC9sJNYAq1U00apBoMFXSYlA

[52] Tristan Claridge, "What is the difference between bonding and bridging social capital?" *Social Capital Research & Training*, website accessed February 3, 2019, https://www.socialcapitalresearch.com/difference-bonding-bridging-social-capital/

[53] David Burkus, "The Wrong Way to Introduce People Over Email," *Harvard Business Review*, October 13, 2016, https://hbr.org/2016/10/the-wrong-way-to-introduce-people-over-email

[54] Jeff Goins, *Real Artists Don't Starve: Timeless Strategies for Thriving in the New Creative Age* (HarperCollins Leadership, 2017.)

[55] Belle Beth Cooper, "How Twitter's Expanded Images Increase Clicks, Retweets and Favorites, *Buffer Social Blog*, updated April 27, 2016, https://blog.bufferapp.com/the-power-of-twitters-new-expanded-images-and-how-to-make-the-most-of-it

[56] Jesse Mawhinney, "45 Visual Content Marketing Statistics You Should Know in 2018, " *Hubspot*, August 17, 2018, https://blog.hubspot.com/marketing/visual-content-marketing-strategy

[57] Inkoo Kang, "Quote of the Day: Shonda Rhimes: I Make TV Look Like the World Looks," *IndieWire*, March 16, 2015, https://www.indiewire.com/2015/03/quote-of-the-day-shonda-rhimes-i-make-tv-look-like-the-world-looks-204266/

[58] Caroline Leach, "6 Ways Social Media Can Help You Prepare for an Initial Business Meeting." Blog. *How to Build Your Career through Social Media*, June 18, 2017, https://www.carolineleach.com/6-ways-social-media-can-help-you-prepare-for-an-initial-business-meeting/

[59] Carly Okyle, "18 Tips to Create Your Perfect LinkedIn Profile," *Entrepreneur*, April 4, 2016, https://www.entrepreneur.com/slideshow/307172#2

[60] Caroline Leach, "What Happens When You Post to LinkedIn Every Weekday for a Month?" Blog. *How to Build Your Career through Social Media*, June 5, 2017, https://www.carolineleach.com/what-happens-when-you-post-to-linkedin-every-weekday-for-a-month/

[61] "LinkedIn Post, Video and Published Article Analytics – Overview," LinkedIn Help website accessed February 3, 2019, https://www.linkedin.com/help/linkedin/answer/83597

[62] Maxwell Gollin, "What Are the Best Times to Post on Social Media in 2019"? Falcon.IO, January 9, 2019, https://www.falcon.io/insights-hub/topics/social-media-management/best-time-to-post-on-social-media-2018/

[63] Liz Rees-Jones, Katherine L. Milkman, Jonah Berger, "The Secret to Online Success: What Makes Content Go Viral," *Scientific American*, April 14, 2015, https://www.scientificamerican.com/article/the-secret-to-online-success-what-makes-content-go-viral/

[64] Seth Stephens-Davidowitz, *Everybody Lies: Big Data, New Data and What the Internet Can Tell Us About Who We Really Are* (New York: HarperCollins, 2017.)

[65] Josh Ochs, *Light, Bright & Polite for Teens/Young Adults*, (Media Leaders, LLC, 2017)

[66] Caroline Leach, "Angelica Kelly Profile: If I Can Do It, You Can Too." Blog. *How to Build Your Career through Social Media*, August 13, 2018, https://www.carolineleach.com/angelica-kelly-profile-if-i-can-do-it-you-can-too/

[67] Caroline Leach, "Why You Should Thank People for Con-

necting on LinkedIn." LinkedIn article, August 2, 2017, https://www.linkedin.com/pulse/why-you-should-thank-people-connecting-linkedin-caroline-leach/

[68] Caroline Leach, "A Love Letter to the Amazing People I've Worked With," LinkedIn article, August 30, 2018, https://www.linkedin.com/pulse/love-letter-amazing-people-ive-worked-caroline-leach/

[69] Jane Friedman, *The Business of Being a Writer*. (Chicago: The University of Chicago Press, 2018.)

[70] Gary Vaynerchuk, "Document, Don't Create: Creating Content That Builds Your Personal Brand," Gary Vaynerchuk website, 2017, https://www.garyvaynerchuk.com/creating-content-that-builds-your-personal-brand/

[71] Chandler Bolt, "How to Turn Pro as a Writer with Jeff Goins," *Self Publishing School* podcast episode 007 posted June 13, 2017, https://self-publishingschool.com/sps-007-art-work-jeff-goins/

[72] Caroline Leach, "Boost Your Career through Social Media, Part 1," Blog. *How to Build Your Career through Social Media*, April 10, 2018, https://www.carolineleach.com/boost-your-career-through-social-media-part-1/

[73] Rachel Samuels, "A complete calendar of hashtag holidays for 2019." Sprout Social Blog. December 17, 2018, https://sproutsocial.com/insights/hashtag-holidays/

[74] Caroline Leach, "What If?" Blog. *How to Build Your Career through Social Media*, October 28, 2016, https://www.carolineleach.com/what-if/

[75] Caroline Leach, "18 Ways to Live Tweet an Event." Blog. *How to Build Your Career through Social Media*, July 29, 2017, https://www.carolineleach.com/18-ways-to-live-tweet-an-event/

[76] Karie Willyerd and Barbara Mistick, *Stretch: How to Future Proof Yourself for Tomorrow's Workplace* (New Jersey: John Wiley & Sons, Inc., 2016.)

[77] Robert Cialdini, Influence: The Psychology of Persuasion. (New York: Harper Collins, 2006.)

[78] Adam Grant, Give and Take: Why Helping Others Drives Our Success. (New York: Penguin Books, 2013.)

[79] Jen McClure, "Employee Advocacy and Social Selling Programs Experience Significant Growth in 2017, According to New Study by JEM Consulting & Advisory Services," News Release, August 23, 2017,

http://www.prweb.com/releases/2017/employee_advocacy/prweb14623270.htm

[80] John Hall, "6 PR Trends to Check Out in 2018," *Forbes*, August 6, 2017, https://www.forbes.com/sites/johnhall/2017/08/06/6-pr-trends-to-check-out-in-2018/#2ab93b846666

[81] Shel Holtz, "What does it take to get employees to keep coming back to your communication app?" Blog. *Communicating at the Intersection of Business and Technology*, January 26, 2017, http://holtz.com/blog/employee-engagement/what-does-it-take-to-get-employees-to-keep-coming-back-to-your-communicatio/4726/

[82] Gary Vaynerchuk, "Document, Don't Create: Creating Content That Builds Your Personal Brand," Gary Vaynerchuk website, 2017, https://www.garyvaynerchuk.com/creating-content-that-builds-your-personal-brand/

[83] Penelope Trunk, "Reach Your Goals by Blogging." Online course through Quistic. 2013. http://www.quistic.com/seminar/reach-your-goals-by-blogging

[84] Guy Kawasaki and Peg Fitzgerald, *The Art of Social Media: Power Tips for Power Users* (New York: Penguin Group, 2014.)

[85] Ashley Judd, "How online abuse of women has spiraled out of control." TED talk. October 2016, https://www.ted.com/talks/ashley_judd_how_online_abuse_of_women_has_spiraled_out_of_control

[86] "58 Incredible and Interesting Twitter Stats," *Brandwatch*, January 3, 2019, https://www.brandwatch.com/blog/twitter-stats-and-statistics/